PASTA IS NOT FATTENING

DELICIOUS RECIPES FOR TODAY'S LIFESTYLE

PASTA IS NOT FATTENING

DELICIOUS RECIPES FOR TODAY'S LIFESTYLE

by **SYLVANA MICILLO VILLATA**

Translation by Jean Bouchard

COVER PICTURE : Les Productions Stanké

PHOTOGRAPHS by Thierry Debeur
with the coordination of Huguette Béraud.

The dishes presented in color have been prepared by Jean-Claude Marchoux
at the restaurant "La vieille École" using Wedgwood plates, Eaton's linen,
the flowers from Charles Alcantara, florist.

Drawings : Christine Mercier

ISBN 2-7604-0225-8

Copyright : 2nd trimester 1984

Printed in Canada

TABLE OF CONTENTS

FOREWORD

There is a new trend in our culture, that of keeping trim and healthy while at the same time indulging in the pleasure of good food.

Pasta, in this respect, is a sure winner. Often shunned in the past for fear of causing weight gain, pasta is now fully appreciated by lovers of good food who *want to stay trim.* Indeed, recent studies have shown that pasta is a food with high nutritional value.

At a time when physical activity is more and more in fashion, each of us needs a diet that supplies enough energy while at the same time allowing for our daily needs in protein.

It is now recognized that the best food balance contains less proteins than previously believed. Proteins are certainly very important for the good health of our tissues and muscles in general, however they are not our best source of energy. Fats also supply energy, but carbohydrates are the most useful because they are digested very easily and assimilated quickly. Our old conception that "steak is the best" is being questioned. Not that steak is not good or good for you, but a more varied choice of fruits and vegetables is recommended, as well as food that is rich in carbohydrates : pasta, bread, cereals, rice and potatoes. So pasta, as you can see, is a great source of energy. Cooked "Italian-style", it makes for a well-balanced meal, helping us to stay trim and healthy.

The recipes we have gathered for this book are at the same time original, tasty and nourishing. Easy to make, pleasing to the eye and delicious to the taste, they will be a delight to all pasta enthusiasts.

Healthy eating need not be at the expense of delicious eating. On the contrary, both go hand in hand. These recipes, I am sure, will convince you.

Yours sincerely,

Claire Hardy
Consumer Services
Catelli

INTRODUCTION

Since doctors and dietitians have demonstrated that pasta has a high nutritional value and is not fattening even when it is eaten regularly, Mediterranean cuisine has offered serious competition to low-calorie diets. Some specialists are even recommending pasta as a weekly part of their menu to patients suffering from obesity. And with positive results !

In light of these facts, how can we explain that pasta has been in disrepute for so long and that it is now suddenly regaining the popularity it deserves ? There are many reasons for this, based on studies conducted by experts.

If we examine the composition of pasta, we will find it contains a number of nourishing ingredients. 100 g (3.5 oz) of pasta made of durum wheat semolina contains approximately :

    10% water
    12% proteins
    75% carbohydrates
         B vitamins
         minerals (phosphorus, calcium, potassium, iron)
         little salt
         very little fat

The presence of carbohydrates, which provide energy that the body can use quickly, is appreciable. As for vitamin B, which is necessary for cellular life and essential for a healthy nervous system, it makes pasta an excellent anti-stress food. It is also good to know that pasta contains very little salt.

But why is Italian-style pasta so special ? Because it is usually served with cheese, the proteins of which complete those of the pasta. The originality of Italian pasta resides mainly in the combination of pasta with the vegetables in season. Tomatoes, almost always present in our recipes, give us vitamins A and C that are not present in pasta alone. Other vegetables such as mushrooms, peas, zucchini, asparagus, green peppers, in addition to containing vitamins and minerals, are also rich in cellulose and hemicellulose, more commonly known as fibers. A diet rich in fibers activates the intestinal tract and facilitates elimination. For these reasons, vegetables are highly appreciated, but they are also enjoyed because of their delicious flavour, brought out in each recipe by a choice of fine herbs and spices.

So for all these reasons, Italian-style pasta is a dish that is an essential part of a well-balanced diet.

Today, whether out of reason or out of passion, pasta has become the "in" food all over America and Europe. Noodles are replacing the traditional potatoes everywhere, in Britain, in Germany, in France.

Statistics show that pasta consumption in Great Britain has tripled in five years and has now reached 2.2 kilos (5 lb) per person per year ; in West Germany, it is 3.3 kilos (7 lb) and in the U.S., 5 kilos (11 lb) while the French eat 7 kilos (15 lb) and the Italians remain comfortably at the top with 27 kilos (59 lb) (*La Presse*, May 4, 1983).

And if the persuasive evidence of specialists is not enough to liberate you from your "pastaphobia", you might let yourself be convinced by the accounts of famous movie stars. Claudia Cardinale, in an interview to the French magazine *L'Express* (January 14, 1983), confessed she preferred lasagne to aerobics : "With pasta, you really lose weight !" To the reporter of the *Figaro* (December 4, 1982), she confided : "Twenty years on a diet ! For twenty years I was an unwilling vegetarian, lettuce-tomatoes, tomatoes-lettuce, twenty years ! And I was gaining weight... I got fed up. I quit and started eating what I liked. And now I am losing weight !" Her secret ? Pasta and couscous.

There is no denying it, the value of pasta has finally been recognized. More so, it is now at the place of honour.

When I decided to write this book, I did not intend it to be a scientific, even less a medical or dietetic work. This simple book was written mainly for those who deprive themselves of a real nutritional benefit out of fear of gaining weight. It is also intended for pasta lovers. To both, I would like to offer these delicious recipes that are no threat to their waistline.

Of course, overeating at every meal will cause you to gain weight, especially if after a tasty pasta entrée, you go on with meat and potatoes, bread and butter followed by a plate of cheese, and at the end, dessert topped with whipped cream.

This book will therefore be useful to those who wish to stay trim without forsaking this nourishing food and those who would like to lose a few pounds without abandoning their favourite dish. Another goal is to prove that low-calorie recipes can also be tasty and that food prepared with light seasoning can be delicious.

If a total number of 1,500 to 2,000 calories a day is allowable, and if your pasta dinner provides you with 400 calories, a very simple calculation will show that the remaining calories can be shared between breakfast and your other meal. This gives you a great deal of latitude for those two meals.

The first part of the book contains low-calorie recipes averaging between 300 and 550 calories per serving. In the second part, you will find more elaborate and richer recipes that you may want to use on special occasions when counting calories is overlooked. They average 650 calories per serving.

Many recipes in this book come from my grandmother. Some of them I remember from my childhood when I used to sit and watch tirelessly her every gesture over the stove. Others I found written down in an old notebook where she kept her personal observations as well as recipes she had heard of from friends. The rest are the result of my own personal experiences. Imagination is useful in everything, especially cooking. There is nothing like a new recipe to turn a simple meal into a real feast. So, after you've tried my recipes, you might want to invent your own. Simply remember these few basic principles :

— Do not add too much salt to your pasta or your sauce ;
— avoid greasy ingredients ; a little olive oil is all right ;
— use a little beef or chicken stock to make the sauce ;
— skim milk yogurt and Ricotta cheese are excellent substitutes for béchamel sauce ;
— vegetables make exquisite sauces ;
— bay leaf, basil, oregano, savory, tarragon, dill and coriander are very appetizing herbs, and you shouldn't hesitate to use them to season your pasta ;
— don't be afraid to use onion and garlic.

By following these simple rules, you are sure to turn every Italian pasta dinner into a real delight, a meal which will be both reasonable and thrilling !

Sylvana Micillo Villata

A WALK THROUGH TIME...

Pasta is said to come from China, first brought to the West by the Venetian navigator Marco Polo in 1292. True fact or legend, the question is still open. One thing is sure, the Chinese have been making a kind of pasta very similar to our spaghetti, although out of soybean flour, for as long as one can remember. Some historians contend that the Egyptians also ate a kind of tubular-shaped pasta resembling our macaroni ; that the Romans were fond of another large, flat variety similar to today's lasagna, while the Etruscans preferred yet another type of pasta in the shape of noodles. As for the pasta that we know today, it first appeared in Genoa in the 13th century. "Maccheroni", the ancestor of present-day macaroni, is first mentioned in a legal document dating back to 1279 and kept in the National Library Archives in Genoa.

Contrary to popular belief, pasta became popular in soutern Italy much later, in the 18th century. In Naples, it soon became the rage. Pasta was eaten everywhere, in inns, at home, even on street benches. It was eaten plain, or sprinkled with a little pepper and Parmesan cheese.

Pasta was not exclusively the common man's fare. The rich and the noble were also very fond of it. Mary of Medici, for instance, feasted on hot, spicy macaroni served to her by an Italian chef at a Parisian inn where she used to go. At the court of Naples, itself, pasta was served to the delight of kings, princes and noblemen. In a document dating back to the end of the XVIIIth century, King Ferdinand regrets not being able to serve pasta during royal court dinners, because good manners forbade eating pasta the way a good peasant would.

In those days, the fork was a rudimentary utensil that made it very difficult to spear the macaroni and roll it into a sizeable mouthful. Luckily, a faithful courtisan of the king quickly came to his aid and offered him a fork with long prongs with which he would be able to feast on his favourite dish in complete dignity before his court.

It was the famous gastronome Thomas Jefferson who, in the late XVIIIth century, imported macaroni from Naples to America. Since then, pasta has been playing an ever-increasing role in our everyday food habits. Indeed, for pasta lovers, a dish of noodles, spaghetti or small shells is always a welcome sight. A friend of mine who often shares my views told me the other day : "When I am happy, I want to eat pasta. When I am depressed, I have to eat pasta. And when I am on a diet, I can't go without pasta".

Don't you feel the same way too ?

NOTE FROM THE PUBLISHER

"The metric system is too complicated" most people believe.

"We must replace the old system by the new" order the authorities. Who are we to pass judgment ? And to prove to you that our main concern is the comfort of our readers, we have presented these delicious recipes both ways. So you can choose.

But beware ! Never mix the two, you may end up with memorable surprises...

LONG MACARONI

MACARONI WITH THREE CHEESES

(4 servings)

340 g	(1 handful 4.5 cm in diameter) Catelli long macaroni	1¾ inches in diameter
125 mL	Ricotta cheese	½ cup
125 mL	chicken stock	½ cup
125 mL	cottage cheese	½ cup
250 mL	milk (2% M.F.)	1 cup
125 mL	feta cheese	½ cup
1	egg, beaten	1

Mix the Ricotta cheese with chicken stock to obtain a light, creamy texture, and put aside.

Mix cottage cheese with a little milk.

Cut the feta cheese into pieces and mix with egg.

Cook the pasta until half-done, and drain.

In a medium-size ovenproof dish, place one third of the pasta, and cover with cottage cheese. Add another third of pasta and cover with Ricotta cheese, covering last layer of pasta with feta cheese and egg mixture. Pour the rest of the milk along the sides of the dish so it will reach the bottom.

Heat oven at 190°C (375°F) and cook macaroni *au gratin* for about 30 minutes. Serve piping hot.

527 calories per serving

MACARONI ANGELICO

(4 servings)

340 g	(1 handful 4.5 cm in diameter) Catelli long macaroni	1¾ inches in diameter
1	medium onion, finely chopped	1
30 mL	olive oil	2 tbsp
200 g	ground veal	7 oz
2	cloves garlic	2
2	small containers (175 g) plain skim milk yogurt	2- 6-5 oz
10 mL	rosemary	2 tsp

Sauté the onion in a little oil. Add veal and cook for 10 minutes over medium heat. Reduce heat and allow to simmer for 10 more minutes.

Meanwhile, prepare sauce. Crush the garlic and add yogurt, a little at a time and mixing well, then add olive oil. Beat quickly to blend all the ingredients.

Cook the pasta in salted boiling water. When it is *al dente,* drain and top with meat and yogurt sauce. Mix quickly and serve hot.

515 calories per serving

SPAGHETTI

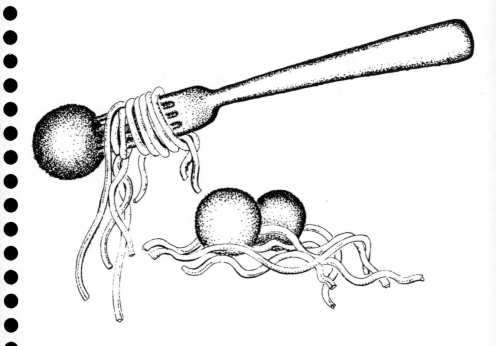

SPAGHETTI MILANESE

(4 servings)

This recipe is light and easy to make. The sauce can be prepared in advance and kept frozen.

340 g	(1 handful 4 cm in diameter) Catelli spaghetti	1½ inches in diameter
1	chopped onion	1
15 mL	olive oil	1 tbsp
250 g	ground veal	½ lb
	salt and pepper to taste	
10 mL	rosemary	2 tsp
5 mL	dry mustard	1 tsp
1	can (540 mL) tomatoes, crushed	1 - 19 oz

Sauté the onion quickly in olive oil and add the meat. Mix well to cook the veal evenly. Add salt, pepper, rosemary and dry mustard. Allow to simmer 15 minutes over low heat, then add the tomatoes. Taste for seasoning. Simmer 10 more minutes then put aside. Cook the spaghetti in salted boiling water. When it is *al dente*, drain and top with meat sauce. Sprinkle with Parmesan cheese if desired.

487 calories per serving

SPAGHETTI RATATOUILLE

(4 servings)

Serve hot or cold according to the season.

340 g	(1 handful 4 cm in diameter) Catelli spaghetti	1½ inches in diameter
4	zucchini, finely chopped	4
1	large green pepper, finely chopped	1
2	cloves garlic, finely chopped	2
15 mL	olive oil	1 tbsp
3	large, fresh tomatoes, diced	3
125 mL	black olives, pitted	½ cup
125 mL	tomato sauce	½ cup
	oregano, parsley and sweet basil, to taste	

Steam the zucchini and green pepper separately, as their cooking time is not the same.

Sauté the garlic in olive oil, then add the cooked vegetables, tomatoes, olives and herbs. Add tomato sauce, and allow to simmer 10 minutes over low heat.

While the sauce is simmering, cook the pasta in salted boiling water. When it is *al dente,* drain well and mix to the sauce.

444 calories per serving

SPAGHETTI RIVIERA

(4 servings)

340 g	(1 handful 4 cm in diameter) Catelli spaghetti	1½ inches in diameter
2	sweet red peppers, very plump	2
6	very ripe tomatoes (or, if not available, 6 canned tomatoes, peeled)	6
1	clove garlic	1
15 mL	olive oil	1 tbsp
5 mL	anchovy paste	1 tsp
15 mL	capers	1 tbsp
5 mL	oregano	1 tsp
125 mL	chicken stock	½ cup

Wash sweet peppers and dry well. Thread the peppers on a skewer or a long fork and roast over flame (or burner if using an electric stove). Turn on all sides to roast the skin evenly, then quickly plunge into cold water. The skin can then be easily removed. Cut the peppers in half lengthwise, remove seeds, and cut in fine slices.

If using fresh tomatoes, soak them in boiling water for one minute, then remove the skin and seeds. Dice.

Sauté the garlic in olive oil until golden. To the same pan, add the tomatoes and sweet peppers, stirring to prevent from sticking. Add one half of the chicken stock, and allow to simmer for 20 minutes.

Meanwhile, mix the anchovy paste, capers and oregano in the remaining half of the chicken stock, and put over low heat. Stir the mixture into the sauce just before serving. Cook the pasta in salted boiling water. When it is *al dente*, drain and serve immediately with the sauce.

405 calories per serving

SPAGHETTI WITH CEPE MUSHROOMS

(4 servings)

340 g	(1 handful 4 cm in diameter) Catelli spaghetti	1½ inches in diameter
1	package (10 g) dried cepe mushrooms	1 - 0.5 oz
250 mL	water	1 cup
175 mL	Ricotta cheese	⅔ cup
	salt and pepper to taste	
½	grated onion	½
15 mL	olive oil	1 tbsp

Soak the dried mushrooms in 250 mL (1 cup) warm water for 1 hour until they are puffed and saturated with water. Remove mushrooms, squeeze out water and put aside. Reserve the water.

In a bowl, soften the Ricotta cheese by adding water from the mushrooms, a little at a time, and mixing until creamy. Add salt and pepper to taste.

Sauté the onion in oil and add the mushrooms. Stir constantly for about two minutes to prevent from sticking. Put aside.

Cook the pasta in salted boiling water. When it is *al dente,* drain and mix with the Ricotta cheese and mushrooms.

Serve piping hot with a dash of ground pepper.

426 calories per serving

SPAGHETTI WITH CHIVES

(4 servings)

340 g	(1 handful 4 cm in diameter) Catelli spaghetti	1½ inches in diameter
50 mL	fresh chives, chopped	¼ cup
4	artichoke hearts, cut in thin slices	4
15 mL	olive oil	1 tbsp
	a little chicken stock	
	salt and pepper to taste	

Sauté the chives and artichokes in olive oil for a few minutes, stirring constantly. Add a little stock if needed, and salt and pepper.

Cook the spaghetti in salted boiling water. When it is very *al dente,* drain and keep warm, and stir in the chives and artichoke mixture.

Serve piping hot.

355 calories per serving

SPAGHETTI WITH CAULIFLOWER

(4 servings)

This recipe can be served hot or cold.

340 g	(1 handful 4 cm in diameter) Catelli spaghetti	1½ inches in diameter
1	small cauliflower	1
4	anchovy fillets	4
125 mL	chicken stock	½ cup
	juice of 1 lemon	1
25 mL	olive oil	1½ tbsp
125 mL	black olives, pitted	½ cup
1	clove garlic, crushed pepper to taste	1

Cook the cauliflower and allow to cool. Cut into small pieces and put aside.

Dissolve the anchovies in chicken stock over very low heat. Add lemon juice, olive oil, garlic and pepper.

Cook the pasta in salted boiling water. When it is *al dente,* drain and top with cauliflower, black olives and sauce.

416 calories per serving

SPAGHETTI WITH HOT PEPPERS

(4 servings)

340 g	(1 handful 4 cm in diameter) Catelli spaghetti	1½ inches in diameter
1	egg	1
25 mL	olive oil	1½ tbsp
	juice of 1 lemon	1
10 mL	chili pepper, crushed	2 tsp
125 mL	grated Pecorino or Romano cheese	½ cup

To prepare the sauce, mix the egg with oil and lemon juice, and beat lightly into a froth. Add chili and put aside.

Meanwhile, cook the pasta in salted boiling water. When it is very *al dente*, drain and put back in cooking pot over low heat.

Quickly add the sauce and cheese. Mix well and serve piping hot.

457 calories per serving

Variation : Garlic may be substituted for chili. Prepare the sauce as directed, then add 3 cloves crushed garlic and 125 mL (½ cup) chopped parsley. Cheese in this case is optional. Parmesan cheese, which is not as sharp, can also be used.

SPAGHETTI WITH MEATBALLS

(4 servings)

340 g	(1 handful 4 cm in diameter) Catelli spaghetti	1½ inches in diameter
200 g	ground veal	½ lb
1	onion	1
1	egg, slightly beaten	1
30 mL	olive oil	2 tbsp
10 mL	rosemary	2 tsp
125 mL	tomatoes, peeled and crushed	½ cup
125 mL	stock	½ cup
30 mL	grated Parmesan cheese salt and pepper to taste	2 tbsp

Grate one half of the onion and mix with ground veal and egg. Roll into little balls.

Coarsely chop other half of onion and fry in olive oil until golden. Season the meatballs with the rosemary, salt and pepper. Add to pan. Turn the meatballs often to brown evenly. If meat sticks to the pan, add a little stock. When the meatballs are done, add the tomatoes and simmer for 10 minutes. Add more stock or a little water, if needed.

Meanwhile, bring salted water to a boil, and cook the pasta *al dente*. Drain and serve with sauce and top with Parmesan cheese.

510 calories per serving

SPAGHETTI WITH RICOTTA CHEESE SAUCE

(4 servings)

340 g	(1 handful 4 cm in diameter) Catelli spaghetti	1½ inches in diameter
150 mL	Ricotta cheese	⅔ cup
50 mL	stock	¼ cup
1	540 mL can tomatoes	1 - 19 oz
1	clove garlic, finely chopped	1
1	medium onion, finely chopped	1
	salt and pepper to taste	
15 mL	olive oil	1 tbsp

Soften the Ricotta cheese in a bowl until creamy, adding a little stock.

Drain the tomatoes and add garlic, onion, salt and pepper. Add olive oil to the tomatoes, mix into a purée and allow to reduce over low heat. Add a little stock, if needed.

Meanwhile, cook the pasta in salted boiling water. When it is *al dente,* drain and put back in the cooking pot. Stir in the tomato sauce and Ricotta cheese. Mix quickly and serve.

Note : This recipe can be stored in the refrigerator for the next day. To serve, simply cook *au gratin* in oven at 180°C (350°F) for 40 minutes.

445 calories per serving

33

SPAGHETTI PRIMAVERA

(4 servings)

340 g	(1 handful 4 cm in diameter) Catelli spaghetti	1½ inches in diameter
1	medium-size onion, finely chopped	1
15 mL	olive oil	1 tbsp
1	stalk celery, diced	1
3	carrots, cut in round slices	3
1	green pepper, finely chopped	1
½	540 mL can of tomatoes	½ - 19 oz
125 mL	chopped parsley	½ cup
5 mL	fresh basil	1 tps, fresh
	or	or
3 mL	dried basil	½ tps, dried
	salt and pepper to taste	

Sauté the onion in olive oil. Add the celery, carrots, green pepper and enough juice from the tomatoes to cook the vegetables. Cover and allow to cook at least 20 minutes over medium heat. Let the vegetables cool and purée them in a blender.

In a saucepan, crush the tomatoes and add the vegetable purée, parsley and basil. Season to taste and allow to simmer 20 minutes.

Meanwhile, cook the pasta in salted boiling water. When it is *al dente*, drain and serve with sauce.

388 calories per serving

SPAGHETTI ALLA PIZZAIOLA

(4 servings)

This recipe is delicious served hot in winter. It is also very refreshing served cold in summer.

340 g	(1 handful 4 cm in diameter) Catelli spaghetti	1½ inches in diameter
1	clove garlic, finely chopped	1
15 mL	olive oil	1 tbsp
1	540 mL can tomatoes, drained	1 - 19 oz
175 mL	black olives, pitted and halved	¾ cup
10 mL	oregano	2 tsp
	salt and pepper to taste	

Sauté the garlic in olive oil until golden. Crush the tomatoes lightly with a fork and add to pan, with the olives. Allow to simmer for 35 minutes over very low heat and at the end, add oregano, salt and pepper.

While the sauce is simmering, cook the pasta in salted boiling water. When it is *al dente,* that is, still firm to the bite, remove from heat and drain.

Put the pasta back into the cooking pot and add the sauce. Cook over low heat for a few minutes while stirring or "tiring" *(mantecare)* the spaghetti to make sure it is well coated with the sauce.

Serve piping hot.

411 calories per serving

35

SPAGHETTI ALLA CAPRESE

(4 servings)

340 g	(1 handful 4 cm in diameter) Catelli spaghetti	1½ inches in diameter
30 mL	parsley	2 tbsp
30 mL	chives	2 tbsp
125 mL	capers	½ cup
30 mL	olive oil	2 tbsp
30 mL	stock	2 tbsp
125 mL	breadcrumbs	½ cup
15 mL	oregano	1 tbsp
250 mL	grated Pecorino or Romano cheese	1 cup
	salt and pepper to taste	

Finely chop the parsley, chives and capers and allow to macerate together in the stock mixed with olive oil.

While pasta is cooking in salted boiling water, brown the breadcrumbs seasoned with oregano in a Teflon frying pan, with no butter or fat. Agitate the pan constantly.

When the spaghetti is cooked *al dente,* drain and stir in capers and herbs. Add salt and pepper, and top with browned breadcrumbs and Pecorino cheese. Serve immediately.

538 calories per serving

SPAGHETTINI

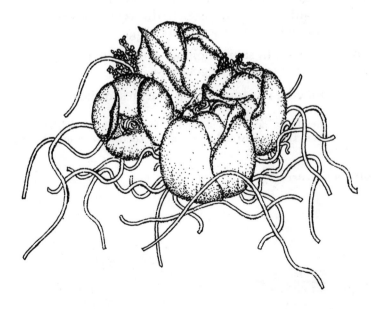

SPAGHETTINI CREOLE

(4 servings)

340 g	(1 handful 4 cm in diameter) Catelli spaghettini	1½ inches in diameter
12	Brussels sprouts	12
300 mL	milk (2% M.F.)	1¼ cups
15 mL	olive oil	1 tbsp
5 mL	ground coriander*	1 tsp
5 mL	onion powder salt and pepper to taste	1 tsp
30 mL	grated Parmesan cheese	2 tbsp

Cook the Brussels sprouts in lightly salted water until half-done. Remove from heat, cut sprouts into pieces and continue cooking in milk over low heat. When the sprouts are done, remove with a skimmer and sauté very quickly in oil. Sprinkle with coriander and onion powder, mix well and add salt and pepper to taste. If the vegetables seem dry, add a little of the milk used in cooking.

Cook the pasta in salted boiling water. When it is *al dente*, drain and mix with the vegetables.

Serve immediately, topped with Parmesan cheese.

* Coriander has a powerful taste and gives a very special flavour to vegetables. If this flavour is not appreciated, savory may be used instead.

419 calories per serving

SPAGHETTINI SORRENTO

(4 servings)

340 g	(1 handful 4 cm in diameter) Catelli spaghettini	1½ inches in diameter
4	anchovy fillets	4
125 mL	chicken stock	½ cup
2	cloves garlic, chopped	2
30 mL	parsley	2 tbsp
30 mL	fresh basil	2 tbsp, fresh
	or	or
15 mL	dried basil	1 tbsp, dried
15 mL	olive oil	1 tbsp
4	fresh tomatoes, diced	4

Dissolve the anchovies in 125 mL (½ cup) chicken stock over very low heat. Add a little more stock if needed. When anchovies are dissolved, remove from heat and allow to cool.

In an electric blender, combine dissolved anchovies with garlic, parsley and basil. Add oil and cook over low heat.

Cook the pasta in boiling water with very little salt added, because anchovies already contain enough salt. When spaghettini is *al dente*, drain and dress with anchovy sauce.

Serve hot, topped with diced tomatoes and a little parsley.

351 calories per serving

VERMICELLI

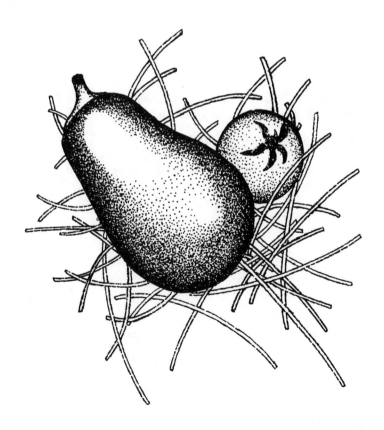

VERMICELLI WITH ALMONDS

(4 servings)

340 g	(1 handful 4 cm in diameter) Catelli long vermicelli	1½ inches in diameter
175 g	green olives ("Sicilian"), pitted and coarsely chopped	¾ cup
125 mL	blanched almonds, coarsely chopped	½ cup
1	egg, beaten with a little water	1
15 mL	olive oil	1 tbsp
1	pinch of ginger	1
15 mL	minced chives	1 tbsp
25 mL	fresh basil, minced or	1½ tbsp, fresh or
10 mL	dried basil	2 tsp, dried
15 mL	minced parsley	1 tbsp
30 mL	grated Parmesan cheese	2 tbsp

Carefully combine the olives, almonds and herbs. Blend in the egg, oil and ginger until mix becomes frothy.

Cook the pasta in salted boiling water. When it is *al dente*, drain and reserve a little of the cooking water. Quickly stir in the olives and almonds, adding a little of the cooking water — about 75 mL (⅓ cup) — so the vermicelli will be well coated with the sauce. Add Parmesan cheese at the very end and serve.

504 calories per serving

VERMICELLI WITH RED SAUCE

(4 servings)

340 g	(1 handful 4 cm in diameter) Catelli long vermicelli	1½ inches in diameter
1	large eggplant, diced	1
250 mL	mushrooms, sliced	1 cup
2	large tomatoes, very ripe	2
1	clove garlic, chopped	1
30 mL	olive oil	2 tbsp
15 mL	fresh basil leaves, minced or	1 tbsp, fresh or
5 mL	dried basil	1 tsp, dried
10 mL	oregano	2 tsp
	salt and pepper to taste	
30 mL	grated Parmesan cheese	2 tbsp

Soak the eggplant in a little salted water for one hour. Do the same with the mushrooms. Drain well and squeeze lightly to remove water. Scald the tomatoes, remove skin and seeds, and crush them with a fork.

Sauté the garlic in oil until golden. Do not allow to brown. Add eggplant, mushrooms, tomatoes, basil, oregano, salt and pepper. Allow to simmer for about 30 minutes over low heat.

Meanwhile, cook the pasta in salted boiling water. When it is *al dente,* drain and dress with the sauce. Mix well and serve immediately, sprinkled with Parmesan cheese or, if you prefer a sharper taste, with Romano cheese.

Variation : Vermicelli can be replaced by rigatoni and cooked in the oven *au gratin* with thin slices of Mozzarella cheese.

434 calories per serving

VERMICELLI PESCATORE

(4 servings)

340 g	(1 handful 4 cm in diameter) Catelli long vermicelli	1½ inches in diameter
250 g	shrimp, shelled	½ lb
500 mL	water	2 cups
1	bay leaf	1
10 mL	garlic powder	2 tsp
30 mL	parsley	2 tbsp
60 mL	olive oil	4 tbsp
10 mL	oregano	2 tsp

Cook the shrimp for 8 minutes over medium heat in about 500 mL (2 cups) water. Add bay leaf and 1 teaspoon garlic powder. When the shrimp are done, remove from heat and drain. Reserve the cooking water.

Chop the parsley and, in an electric blender, combine with the remaining teaspoon of garlic powder, the oil and a little of the cooking water. Add a little water if needed. Stir in the shrimp, whole or cut into pieces if preferred, and keep warm over low heat.

Cook the pasta in salted boiling water. When it is *al dente,* drain and mix with the sauce. Sprinkle with oregano.

489 calories per serving

VERMICELLI WITH CLAM SAUCE

(4 servings)

340 g	(1 handful 4 cm in diameter) Catelli long vermicelli	1½ inches in diameter
3	cloves garlic, finely chopped	3
30 mL	olive oil	2 tbsp
1	can (140 g) small clams pepper to taste	1 - 5 oz
5 mL	chives, finely chopped	1 tsp
5 mL	oregano	1 tsp
125 mL	chopped parsley	½ cup

Sauté the garlic in oil over low heat until it starts turning golden. Drain the clams, keeping the water for later use, and add to pan. Quickly stir for a few minutes, then add 30 mL (2 tbsp) of the clam water. Add the pepper, chives and oregano.

Cook the vermicelli in salted boiling water. When it is *al dente,* top with clam sauce and mix well.

Serve with plenty of parsley.

403 calories per serving

VERMICELLI CATANESI

(4 servings)

340 g	(1 handful 4 cm in diameter) Catelli long vermicelli	1½ inches in diameter
30 mL	olive oil	2 tbsp
2	cloves garlic	2
2	medium eggplants, diced	2
6	fresh tomatoes, diced	6
125 mL	sliced mushrooms	½ cup
1	sweet red pepper, finely sliced	1
10 mL	fresh basil or	2 tsp, fresh or
5 mL	dried basil salt and pepper to taste	1 tsp, dried
10 mL	oregano	2 tsp
30 mL	grated Parmesan cheese	2 tbsp

Sauté the garlic cloves in oil over low heat until golden, then remove from pan and discard. To the same pan, add the eggplants, tomatoes, mushrooms and sweet pepper. Add basil, salt, pepper and oregano. Cover and allow to simmer for 30 minutes over very low heat.

While the sauce is simmering, cook the pasta in salted boiling water. When the pasta is still firm to the bite, drain well and put back into the cooking pot over low heat. Add the sauce and mix well so that the vermicelli is well coated with the sauce. Serve with Parmesan cheese or, for a sharper taste, with Parmesan mixed with Pecorino cheese.

495 calories per serving

LINGUINE

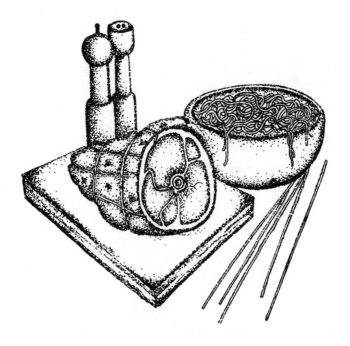

LINGUINE MARINARA

(4 servings)

340 g	(1 handful 4 cm in diameter) Catelli linguine	1½ inches in diameter
3	dozen mussels	3 dozen
250 mL	water	1 cup
2	cloves garlic	2
1	bay leaf	1
25 mL	olive oil	1½ tbsp
15 mL	parsley	1 tbsp
	salt and pepper to taste	
2	fresh tomatoes, diced	2

Clean the mussels well and cook in water with garlic and bay leaf. When the mussels are done (approx. 5 minutes), remove meat from shells and reserve the cooking water.

Meanwhile, cook the pasta *al dente*. Drain and put back on heat. Add the mussels, a little cooking water, the olive oil, parsley, salt, pepper and tomatoes.

Serve immediately.

453 calories per serving

Spaghetti Ratatouille (page 25)
Linguine Marinara (page 48)

LINGUINE AND HERBS

(4 servings)

340 g	(1 handful 4 cm in diameter) Catelli linguine	1½ inches in diameter
30 mL	fresh chives	2 tbsp
30 mL	parsley	2 tbsp
30 mL	fresh basil or	2 tbsp, fresh or
15 mL	dried basil	1 tbsp, dried
3	egg yolks, hard-boiled	3
250 mL	chicken stock	1 cup
25 mL	olive oil	1½ tbsp
250 mL	grated Parmesan cheese salt and pepper to taste	1 cup

Finely chop the herbs together.

In a crock, make a sauce by crushing the egg yolks with a fork, adding stock little by little and mixing swiftly. When mixture becomes creamy, add the olive oil, herbs and Parmesan cheese.

Cook the linguine in salted boiling water. When it is *al dente,* drain and dress with the sauce. Add salt and pepper to taste.

Mix well and quickly, sprinkle with freshly ground pepper and serve hot.

538 calories per serving

Rigatoni with Broccoli (page 67)
Butterflies Cacciatora (page 77)

LINGUINE WITH FENNEL

(4 servings)

340 g	(1 handful 4 cm in diameter) Catelli linguine	1½ inches in diameter
1	stalk fennel	1
25 mL	olive oil	1½ tbsp
	salt and pepper to taste	
5 mL	oregano	1 tsp
1	egg, slightly beaten	1
125 mL	grated Parmesan cheese	½ cup

Cut the fennel into medium-sized pieces and steam in very little water. Drain and sauté in olive oil. Add salt, pepper and oregano.

Mix Parmesan cheese and egg and put aside.

Cook the pasta in salted boiling water. When it is *al dente*, drain and put back in cooking pot. Top with fennel and egg mix, and put over heat for a few seconds to melt the cheese.

Serve hot with a dash of freshly ground pepper.

482 calories per serving

LINGUINE WITH SAFFRON

(4 servings)

340 g	(1 handful 4 cm in diameter) Catelli linguine	1½ inches in diameter
50 mL	Ricotta cheese	¼ cup
125 mL	chicken stock	½ cup
5 mL	onion powder	1 tsp
2 mL	saffron	½ tsp
	salt and pepper to taste	
100 g	lean ham	3.5 oz
30 mL	grated Parmesan cheese	2 tbsp

Mix stock with Ricotta cheese to obtain a light, creamy texture. Add onion powder, saffron, salt and pepper.

Coarsely chop the ham and put aside.

Cook the pasta in salted boiling water. When it is *al dente*, drain and top with the saffron sauce, chopped ham and Parmesan cheese.

Serve immediately.

399 calories per serving

LINGUINE PESTO

(4 servings)

340 g	(1 handful 4 cm in diameter) Catelli linguine	1½ inches in diameter
150 mL	sweet basil leaves or	⅔ cup, fresh or
60 mL	dried basil	4 tbsp, dried
6	cloves garlic, coarsely chopped	6
125 mL	grated Romano cheese	½ cup
75 mL	chicken stock	⅓ cup
75 mL	olive oil salt and pepper to taste	⅓ cup

Put the basil leaves in an electric blender with the garlic, cheese and chicken stock. Blend well. Pour the oil in a light stream with blender running. The sauce is ready when it starts to thicken slightly.

Cook the pasta in salted boiling water. When it is *al dente,* drain and keep a little of the cooking water. Dress with the sauce and serve with a dash of freshly ground pepper.

Note : This sauce can be kept in the freezer without losing its flavour. Simply pour the sauce in an ice cube container. When the sauce is frozen, remove from container and wrap each cube in aluminum foil, then put back in the freezer. Each cube equals one portion. When serving, remove from freezer as many cubes as there are guests to be served, and allow to thaw over very low heat. For a thinner sauce, add one or two tablespoons of the water used to cook the pasta.

537 calories per serving

LINGUINE TRICOLOUR

(4 servings)

This recipe makes for a light, refreshing and tasty meal. It can be served as well in summer as in winter.

340 g	(1 handful 4 cm in diameter) Catelli linguine	1½ inches in diameter
2	cloves garlic, coarsely chopped	2
15 mL	olive oil	1 tbsp
5	tomatoes, diced	5
125 mL	chicken stock	½ cup
	salt and pepper to taste	
5 mL	oregano	1 tsp
125 mL	chopped parsley	½ cup

Sauté the garlic in oil. Add the tomatoes and allow to simmer for 5 minutes, mixing well. Add the stock. Add salt, pepper, oregano and parsley just before removing from heat.

Cook the pasta in salted boiling water. When it is *al dente,* drain and serve with the sauce, decorating each plate with a few sprigs of fresh parsley.

379 calories per serving

53

LINGUINE CAVOUR

(4 servings)

340 g	(1 handful 4 cm in diameter) Catelli linguine	1½ inches in diameter
250 mL	milk (2% M.F.)	1 cup
1	package (155 g) of 2 smoked trout fillets	1 - 10.5 oz
1	small onion, grated	1
15 mL	olive oil	1 tbsp
150 mL	Ricotta cheese diluted in 15 mL milk	⅔ cup - 1 tbsp
	pepper to taste	
5 mL	capers	1 tsp
15 mL	parsley, finely chopped	1 tbsp

Heat milk to the boiling point and pour over trout fillets in a bowl. Let stand about 10 minutes. This will remove excess salt from the trout.

In a frying pan, sauté the grated onion in olive oil over low heat. Pat dry the trout fillets and cut into small pieces. Add to pan, with the Ricotta cheese. Sprinkle with pepper, cover and allow to simmer for 15 minutes over low heat.

Meanwhile, cook the linguine in salted boiling water. When it is *al dente,* drain and put back into cooking pot. Pour in trout and stir very lightly.

Decorate with a few capers and parsley and serve immediately.

534 calories per serving

FETTUCINE

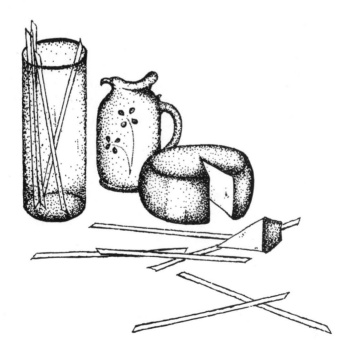

FETTUCINE WITH ZUCCHINI

(4 servings)

340 g	(1 handful 4 cm in diameter) Catelli fettucine	1½ inches in diameter
4	medium zucchini	4
15 mL	unsalted butter	1 tbsp
	salt and pepper to taste	
2	eggs	2
30 mL	milk (2% M.F.)	2 tbsp
30 mL	grated Parmesan cheese	2 tbsp

Carefully wash and pat dry the zucchini, and remove some of the peel so they will not taste bitter. Dice and sauté in butter. Add salt and pepper. When the zucchini are brown, lower heat, cover and cook for 15 more minutes.

Meanwhile, cook the pasta in salted boiling water. While it is cooking, beat the eggs with a little milk, as for an omelet, and pour over zucchini. Stir quickly and remove from heat. When the pasta is *al dente*, drain and serve with the zucchini sauce, topped with Parmesan cheese. Serve piping hot.

431 calories per serving

NOODLES

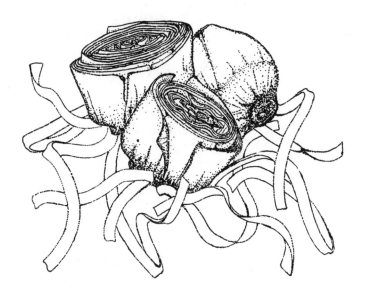

NOODLES FLORENTINE

(4 servings)

340 g	(1.5 L) Catelli medium noodles	6½ cups
1	leek, finely chopped	1
5	artichoke hearts, finely chopped	5
30 mL	olive oil	2 tbsp
125 mL	stock	½ cup
	salt and pepper to taste	
1	clove garlic, finely chopped	1
½	package (284 g) fresh spinach	½ - 10 oz
100 mL	Ricotta cheese	⅓ cup

Sauté the leek and artichoke hearts in half of the olive oil. Add a little stock, salt and pepper, and continue to cook over very low heat.

In another pan, sauté the garlic in the remaining oil. Do not allow to brown. Wash and coarsely chop the spinach, add to pan and stir very quickly. Add salt and pepper. Remove from heat while spinach is still firm.

Mix Ricotta cheese with a little stock to obtain a light, creamy texture.

Meanwhile, cook the noodles in salted boiling water. When they are *al dente,* drain carefully and stir in vegetables and Ricotta cheese. Serve hot, sprinkled with a little grated Pecorino cheese if desired.

461 calories per serving

FARAONA NOODLE CASSEROLE

(4 servings)

340 g	(1.5 L) Catelli egg noodles	6½ cups
2	chicken breasts	2
750 mL	water	3 cups
1	carrot	1
1	stalk celery	1
1	medium onion	1
75 mL	Ricotta cheese	⅓ cup
	salt and pepper to taste	
250 mL	mushrooms, thinly sliced	1 cup
1	pinch nutmeg	1

Remove skin from chicken breasts and cook over medium heat for about 45 minutes in 750 mL (3 cups) water, with the carrot, celery and onion. When the chicken is well cooked and tender, allow to cool, then remove bones and cut into small pieces. Put aside and keep the stock for later use.

To prepare the sauce, mix Ricotta cheese with enough stock to obtain a light, creamy texture. Add the salt, pepper, mushrooms and nutmeg. Stir the pieces of chicken into the sauce, cover and allow to simmer for 15 minutes over low heat.

Meanwhile, cook the pasta in salted boiling water. When it is *al dente,* drain and stir into the chicken sauce over very low heat.

Serve immediately.

429 calories per serving

BLACK FOREST NOODLES

(4 servings)

340 g	(1.5 L) Catelli egg noodles	6½ cups
1	package (10 g) dried cepe mushrooms	1 - 0.5 oz
250 mL	water	1 cup
50 g	Black Forest ham	2 oz
50 g	cooked ham	2 oz
50 g	Ricotta cheese	2 oz
½	grated onion	½
15 mL	olive oil	1 tbsp

Soak the dried mushrooms in water for about one hour. Drain and keep the water.

Coarsely chop both types of ham.

Make a light sauce by mixing the Ricotta cheese with the water used to soak the mushrooms.

In a frying pan, sauté the onion in oil until golden, then add the mushrooms and mix well to prevent from sticking. Lower heat to minimum.

Cook the noodles in salted boiling water. When they are *al dente,* drain and mix with other ingredients. Put back on heat for a few seconds, carefully blending the sauce, mushrooms, ham and noodles.

Serve piping hot on warm plates.

442 calories per serving

NOODLES WITH ASPARAGUS SAUCE

(4 servings)

This very delicate recipe is suited for people who count their calories as well as for those who don't. The latter may add a little fresh cream to the sauce.

340 g	(1.5 L) Catelli medium noodles	6½ cups
1	can (341 mL) asparagus, drained	1 - 12 oz
125 mL	chicken stock	½ cup
3	slices lean ham, chopped	3
1	onion, finely chopped	1
15 mL	olive oil	1 tbsp
30 mL	grated Parmesan cheese	2 tbsp
	salt and pepper to taste	

In an electric blender, combine the chicken stock, asparagus and chopped ham to obtain a purée. Add a little stock if needed. Add salt and pepper to taste.

In a frying pan, sauté the onion in oil over low heat. When onion is golden, add the purée and allow to simmer slowly. If the sauce gets too thick, add a little more stock.

Meanwhile, cook the pasta in salted boiling water. When pasta is done and still firm to the bite *(al dente)*, drain and mix with the sauce.

Serve piping hot with a little Parmesan cheese. Decorate each plate with a few asparagus tips.

417 calories per serving

NOODLES WITH SNOW PEAS

(4 servings)

340 g	(1.5 L) Catelli medium egg noodles	6½ cups
200 g	snow peas	½ lb
30 mL	olive oil	2 tbsp
250 mL	chicken stock	1 cup
2 mL	ground coriander	½ tsp
	salt and pepper to taste	
60 mL	grated Parmesan cheese	4 tbsp

Wash the peas, remove strings and cook for 10 minutes in lightly salted water. Drain well and sauté in olive oil. Add coriander and one half of the stock to the pan. Cover and allow to simmer for about 12 minutes. Add a little stock, if needed.

Meanwhile, cook the pasta in salted boiling water. When it is *al dente,* drain and mix with the peas. Serve hot, sprinkled with Parmesan cheese.

407 calories per serving

MARINATED NOODLES

(4 servings)

340 g	(1.5 L) Catelli egg noodles	6½ cups
	juice of 3 lemons	3
45 mL	olive oil	3 tbsp
	salt and pepper to taste	
5 mL	dried basil	1 tsp
5 mL	celery powder	1 tsp
8	cherry tomatoes	8
15 mL	parsley, finely chopped	1 tbsp

In a bowl, mix the lemon juice and olive oil and beat vigorously. Add salt, pepper, basil and celery powder, and put aside.

Wash the cherry tomatoes, dry and cut in halves.

Cook the noodles in salted boiling water. When they are *al dente*, stir in lemon sauce.

Garnish with tomatoes and parsley, and serve.

448 calories per serving

NOODLES WITH ARTICHOKES

(4 servings)

340 g	(1.5 L) Catelli plain or egg noodles	6½ cups
1	onion, coarsely chopped	1
2	398 mL cans artichoke hearts	2 - 14 oz
15 mL	olive oil	1 tbsp
125 mL	chicken stock	½ cup
125 mL	Ricotta cheese	½ cup
	salt and pepper to taste	
5 mL	ground nutmeg	1 tsp
30 mL	grated Parmesan cheese	2 tbsp

Sauté the onion in oil. Cut the artichokes into small pieces and add to pan, mixing well. Add a little stock if needed, cover and allow to simmer.

Mix Ricotta cheese with remaining stock to obtain a light, creamy texture. Pour over artichokes, add salt and pepper to taste and nutmeg. Reduce heat, cover and allow to simmer for 15 minutes.

Cook the noodles in salted boiling water. When they are *al dente,* drain and put back in cooking pot.

Pour artichoke sauce over noodles, stir well and serve hot with Parmesan cheese.

455 calories per serving

RIGATONI

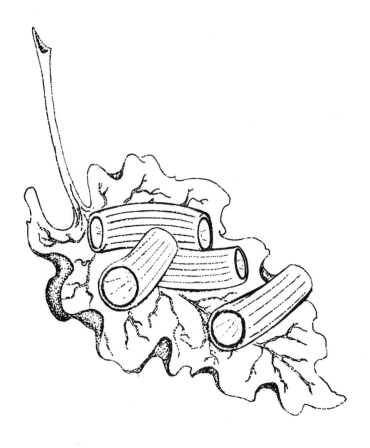

FARMER'S RIGATONI

(4 servings)

This recipe is deliciously spicy.

300 g	(1 L) Catelli rigatoni	4¼ cups
250 mL	beet leaves	1 cup
250 mL	spinach	1 cup
2	cloves garlic, finely chopped	2
30 mL	olive oil	2 tbsp
	chili pepper, to taste	
	salt, to taste	
30 mL	grated Pecorino cheese	2 tbsp

Steam the vegetables in very little water until half-done, then remove from heat and drain.

Sauté the garlic in olive oil seasoned   with chili until golden. Add the vegetables and stir quickly to blend flavours.

Meanwhile, cook the pasta in salted boiling water. When it is *al dente,* drain and top with the vegetables, sprinkled with Pecorino cheese.

355 calories per serving

RIGATONI WITH BROCCOLI

(4 servings)

300 g	(1 L) Catelli rigatoni	4¼ cups
1	medium onion, grated	1
30 mL	olive oil	2 tbsp
750 mL	broccoli, cut into large pieces	3 cups
5 mL	Italian seasonning	1 tsp
60 mL	grated Parmesan cheese	4 tbsp
	salt and pepper to taste	

Cook the broccoli for about 5 minutes in boiling water, until it is tender but still firm.

Sauté the onion in olive oil until golden, then add brocoli and mix quickly. If vegetables stick to the pan, add a little chicken stock. Add Italian seasoning, salt and pepper. Cover and allow to simmer for 5 minutes over low heat.

Meanwhile, cook the rigatoni in salted boiling water. When it is *al dente*, drain and put back in cooking pot over very low heat. Add broccoli, mixing very carefully so not to break the pasta.

Serve hot, sprinkled with Parmesan cheese.

413 calories per serving

STUFFED RIGATONI AND HERBS AU GRATIN

(4 servings)

This recipe takes a little extra time but is very easy to make and is so delicious !

300 g	(1 L) Catelli rigatoni	4¼ cups
15 mL	chopped parsley	1 tbsp
15 mL	dried basil	1 tbsp
15 mL	sage	1 tbsp
5 mL	oregano	1 tsp
175 mL	Ricotta cheese	¾ cup
1	small onion, grated	1
1	large onion, finely chopped	1
	salt and pepper to taste	
1	can (796 mL) tomatoes, drained and crushed	1 - 28 oz
30 mL	olive oil	2 tbsp
60 mL	grated Parmesan cheese	4 tbsp

Mix the herbs together with 15 mL (1 tbsp) water so mixture will not be too dry. Add Ricotta cheese and the grated onion and mix well to obtain a smooth, creamy texture, creamy enough to go through a pastry decorator tube. Add milk (2% M.F.) if needed. Keep in the refrigerator.

To make sauce, sauté the chopped onion in olive oil until golden, then add the tomatoes with salt and pepper.Cover and allow to simmer for 15 minutes.

Cook the pasta until only half-done. The rigatoni must be quite firm to the bite. Rinse under cold water and drain. Using a pastry decorator tube, fill each rigatoni with the cheese mix. Place the stuffed rigatoni side by side in a large rectangular ovenproof dish. Add the tomato sauce and sprinkle with Parmesan cheese, and cook *au gratin* in a pre-heated oven at 190°C (375°F), covered with aluminum foil, for 40 minutes. Remove foil for the last 10 minutes.

508 calories per serving

COUNTRY-STYLE RIGATONI

(4 servings)

This recipe can be served cold during the summer season.

300 g	(1 L) Catelli rigatoni	4¼ cups
4	medium zucchini, cut in very thin round slices	4
500 mL	water	2 cups
2	cloves garlic, crushed	2
30 mL	olive oil	2 tbsp
15 mL	oregano	1 tbsp
150 mL	feta cheese	⅔ cup
150 mL	cottage cheese	⅔ cup
	salt and pepper to taste	
30 mL	grated Parmesan cheese	2 tbsp

Sauté the garlic in olive oil while cooking the zucchini in water. When almost done, drain and add to the frying pan. Add the oregano, salt and pepper. Cover and allow to simmer about 10 minutes.

Combine feta and cottage cheeses together, and put aside.

Cook the pasta in salted boiling water. When it is *al dente*, drain and put back in pot over low heat, quickly mixing in the zucchini and the cheese.

Sprinkle with Parmesan cheese and freshly ground pepper, if desired.

519 calories per serving

RIGATONI LUMBERJACK

(4 servings)

300 g	(1 L) Catelli rigatoni	4¼ cups
1	package (10 g) dried cepe mushrooms	1 - 0.5 oz
250 mL	water	1 cup
1	medium onion, finely chopped	1
30 mL	olive oil	2 tbsp
7	very ripe tomatoes, diced (crushed if using canned tomatoes)	7
	salt and pepper to taste	
100 g	lean smoked ham	3.5 oz
60 mL	grated Parmesan cheese	4 tbsp
1	bunch of parsley, finely chopped	1

Soak the dried mushrooms for about 1 hour in 250 mL (1 cup) water.

Sauté the onion in oil and add the mushrooms, well drained, and the tomatoes. Add salt and pepper, cover, and allow to simmer for 20 minutes. Add a little water from the mushrooms if needed.

Finely chop the ham and put aside.

Cook the rigatoni in salted boiling water. When it is *al dente,* drain and dress with the sauce. Add ham, mix well and quickly. Serve with Parmesan cheese and parsley.

489 calories per serving

71

RIGATONI MARQUISE

(4 servings)

300 g	(1 L) Catelli rigatoni	4¼ cups
1	clove garlic, finely chopped	1
15 mL	olive oil	1 tbsp
375 mL	fresh spinach, chopped	1½ cups
175 mL	Ricotta cheese	¾ cups
30 mL	chicken stock	2 tbsp
10 mL	oregano	2 tsp
	salt and pepper to taste	

Sauté the garlic in olive oil. Wash and pat dry the spinach, and add to pan. Cover and allow to simmer for a few minutes. Spinach must remain crisp.

Meanwhile, mix the Ricotta cheese with the stock to obtain a light, creamy texture. Add oregano, salt and pepper.

Cook the pasta in salted boiling water. When it is *al dente*, drain and put back in cooking pot. Pour the cheese sauce and the spinach over the pasta and put back over low heat for 2 minutes, mixing well.

Serve piping hot.

336 calories per serving

GREEK-STYLE RIGATONI

(4 servings)

320 g	(1 L) Catelli rigatoni	4¼ cups
60 mL	olive paste (see below)	4 tbsp
30 mL	grated Parmesan cheese	2 tbsp

Olive paste :

30 mL	Ricotta cheese	2 tbsp
250 mL	black olives, pitted	1 cup
15 mL	fresh basil, minced	1 tbsp, fresh
	or	or
5 mL	dried basil	1 tsp, dried
2	cloves garlic,chopped (optional)	2

Combine ingredients needed for olive paste in an electric blender, adding a little cold water. Texture must be that of a light cream, not too thick. Put aside.

Cook the rigatoni in salted boiling water. When it is *al dente*, drain and dress with the olive paste and a little cooking water. Serve immediately with Parmesan cheese.

Note : Leftover olive paste makes a delicious dip for raw, crisp vegetables.

327 calories per serving

BOWS

BOWS WITH GREEN VEGETABLES

(4 servings)

300 g	(1,2 L) Catelli medium bows	5¼ cups
1	large onion, finely chopped	1
30 mL	olive oil	2 tbsp
3	leeks, coarsely chopped	3
1	package (284 g) spinach, coarsely chopped	1 - 10 oz
	salt and pepper to taste	
	a little skim milk	
5 mL	oregano	1 tsp
150 mL	grated Parmesan cheese	⅔ cup

Sauté the onion in olive oil, then add leeks and spinach that you have washed and chopped. Add salt and pepper, and a little milk. Cover and allow to simmer for about 15 minutes over low heat.

Meanwhile, cook the pasta in salted boiling water. When it is *al dente,* drain well and mix with the vegetables, and season with oregano. Serve hot with Parmesan cheese.

494 calories per serving

BUTTERFLIES CACCIATORA

(4 servings)

270 g	(1 L) Catelli large bows	4 cups
2	chicken breasts	2
250 mL	stock	1 cup
2	medium onions	2
1	carrot	1
1	stalk celery, diced	1
1	bay leaf	1
15 mL	olive oil	1 tbsp
1	large green pepper, finely sliced	1
1	can (540 mL) tomatoes, drained	1 - 19 oz
	salt and pepper to taste	
10 mL	oregano	2 tsp
5 mL	dry mustard	1 tsp
30 mL	wine vinegar	2 tbsp

Remove skin and bones from chicken breasts. Cook, well covered with water, with one onion and the carrot, celery and bay leaf. When chicken is done (about 20 minutes) allow to cool, then cut into small pieces. Allow stock to cool, remove excess fat, strain and put aside.

In a frying pan, heat the oil and sauté the other onion, finely chopped, until golden. Then add the green pepper, tomatoes, salt, pepper and oregano. Allow to simmer for about 20 minutes, adding a little stock if needed. Stir in the pieces of chicken, the mustard and vinegar, and allow to simmer for about 15 more minutes.

Meanwhile, cook the pasta in salted boiling water. When it is *al dente,* drain and serve with the sauce.

401 calories per serving

SMALL PENS

SMALL PENS AU GRATIN

(4 servings)

320 g	(750 mL) Catelli small pens	3 cups
15 mL	butter or margarine	1 tbsp
15 mL	breadcrumbs	1 tbsp
250 mL	Gruyère, in fine slices	1 cup
100 mL	milk (2% M.F.)	⅓ cup

Cook the pasta in salted boiling water. When it is half-cooked, drain and put aside.

Lightly grease an ovenproof dish, sprinkle with breadcrumbs and pour enough pasta to cover bottom of dish. Then cover pasta with thin slices of Gruyère and small dots of butter or margarine. Alternate layers of pasta and cheese, topping with coarsely grated cheese.

Pour cold milk carefully along the sides of the dish so it will reach the bottom.

Cook *au gratin* in oven at 190°C (375°F) about 30 minutes. Serve piping hot.

457 calories per serving

SMALL PENS WITH DILL

(4 servings)

300 g	(750 mL) Catelli small pens	3 cups
150 mL	Ricotta cheese	2/3 cup
125 mL	milk (2% M.F.)	1/2 cup
1	small onion, finely chopped	1
15 mL	olive oil	1 tbsp
75 mL	fresh dill	1/3 cup
	salt and pepper to taste	

Mix Ricotta cheese with milk and beat vigorously to obtain a light texture.

In a frying pan, sauté the onion in oil over low heat until golden. Add Ricotta cheese and a little more milk if needed. Add dill. Mix well, add salt and pepper and allow to simmer for 15 minutes over very low heat.

Meanwhile, cook the pasta. When it is *al dente,* drain and put back in cooking pot, after pouring in the dill sauce. Mix quickly and serve piping hot on warm plates.

Do not allow the sauce to curdle, as it would spoil this very delicate recipe.

394 calories per serving

SMALL PENS "FRA DIAVOLO"

(4 servings)

This recipe is a little on the spicy side.

300 g	(650 mL) Catelli small pens	2¾ cups
2	medium onions, finely sliced	2
1	clove garlic, crushed	1
30 mL	olive oil	2 tbsp
375 mL	tomatoes, peeled and crushed	1½ cups
25 mL	fresh basil, minced	1½ tbsp , fresh
	or	or
10 mL	dried basil	2 tsp , dried
10 mL	chili	2 tsp
60 mL	grated Pecorino cheese	4 tbsp

Sauté onions and garlic in oil until golden. Add the tomatoes, basil, chili and cheese. Cover and allow to simmer for about 30 minutes over low heat.

Meanwhile, cook the pasta in salted boiling water. When it is *al dente,* drain and put back in cooking pot over low heat. Add the sauce and mix well for about 30 seconds.

Serve hot with plenty of Pecorino cheese.

394 calories per serving

SMALL PENS WITH TUNA

(4 servings)

300 g	(750 mL) Catelli small pens	3 cups
1	chopped onion	1
15 mL	olive oil	1 tbsp
250 mL	medium-sized peas	1 cup
1	can (184 g) tuna	1 - 6.5 oz
125 mL	chicken stock	½ cup
250 mL	tomatoes, peeled and crushed	1 cup
5 mL	oregano	1 tsp

Sauté the onion in olive oil until golden. Add the peas, well drained, the tuna, its excess oil removed by rinsing a few seconds in warm water, and the tomatoes. Add oregano, cover and allow to simmer for 15 minutes over low heat.

Meanwhile, cook the pasta in salted boiling water. When it is very *al dente,* drain and put back in cooking pot. Pour the tuna sauce over the pasta, over low heat, and mix well.

Serve immediately.

448 calories per serving

SHELLS

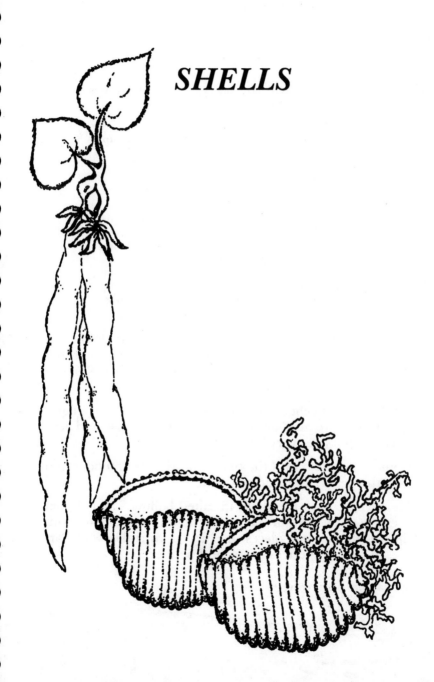

SHELLS WITH SAUCE FINANCIÈRE

(4 servings)

300 g	(1 L) Catelli large shells	4½ cups
2	chicken breasts	2
	court-bouillon :	
250 mL	water	1 cup
1	small onion	1
1	carrot	1
1	stalk celery	1
150 mL	Ricotta cheese	⅔ cup
15 mL	onion powder	1 tbsp
15 mL	tarragon	1 tbsp
	salt and pepper to taste	
125 mL	canned small peas, drained	½ cup
125 mL	carrots, diced	½ cup
30 mL	grated Parmesan cheese	2 tbsp

Remove skin from chicken breasts. Allow to simmer in court-bouillon for about 45 minutes. When chicken is well done, remove from cooking pot and allow to cool. Remove bones and cut into small pieces.

Mix the Ricotta cheese with chicken stock to obtain a light, creamy texture. Add onion powder, tarragon, salt and pepper, and put over very low heat.

Cook the carrots with the onion powder until tender and heat the peas. Drain and put aside.

Meanwhile, cook the shells in salted boiling water. When they are *al dente*, drain and serve with the sauce, mixed with the vegetables and pieces of chicken. Sprinkle with Parmesan cheese and freshly ground pepper.

450 calories per serving

SMALL SHELLS WITH GREEN BEANS

(4 servings)

This recipe is delicious in summer, served as a first course or a salad.

320 g	(650 mL) Catelli small shells	2¾ cups
250 g	green beans	½ lb
25 mL	olive oil	1½ tbsp
25 mL	lemon juice	1½ tbsp
	salt and pepper to taste	
125 mL	Mozzarella cheese, diced	½ cup

Cook the beans in boiling water until tender, drain carefully and cut into two or three pieces if they are very long. Carefully stir in the olive oil and lemon juice. Add salt and pepper to taste, and the cheese.

Cook the pasta in salted boiling water. When it is *al dente*, drain and serve with the beans.

429 calories per serving

SMALL SHELLS WITH TARRAGON SAUCE

(4 servings)

300 g	(650 mL) Catelli small shells	2¾ cups
2	eggs	2
75 mL	milk (2% M.F.)	⅓ cup
125 mL	fresh tarragon, minced	½ cup, fresh
	or	or
30 mL	dried tarragon	2 tbsp, dried
125 mL	grated Parmesan cheese	½ cup

This easy-to-make recipe is very delicate. However, it must be served on warm plates to prevent the sauce from curdling.

Beat the eggs vigorously with milk. Carefully mix in the tarragon. Add the Parmesan cheese a little at a time to prevent sauce from going lumpy. Add a little more milk if needed. Add salt and pepper to taste.

Cook the pasta in salted boiling water. When it is *al dente*, put back in pot over low heat and pour in the sauce. Mix very quickly.

Serve immediately.

386 calories per serving

MACARONI

SPRINGTIME MACARONI

(4 servings)

350 g	(750 mL) Catelli ready-cut macaroni	3 cups
3	cloves garlic, finely chopped	3
200 g	lamb, cut into small pieces	½ lb
15 mL	olive oil	1 tbsp
75 mL	beef stock	⅓ cup
15 mL	chopped mint leaves	1 tbsp

In a frying pan, sauté the garlic and veal in olive oil until meat is browned. Add stock and allow to simmer for 15 minutes. Add salt, pepper and mint.

Cook the pasta in salted boiling water. When it is *al dente*, drain and put back in cooking pot. Add sauce and mix well.

Serve piping hot and decorate with mint leaves.

516 calories per serving

MACARONI WITH HERBS

(4 servings)

320 g	(600 mL) Catelli ready-cut macaroni	2½ cups
30 mL	fresh basil or	2 tbsp , fresh or
15 mL	dried basil	1 tbsp, dried
30 mL	fresh chives, chopped	2 tbsp
15 mL	Ricotta cheese diluted in a little milk (2% M.F.)	1 tbsp
30 mL	lemon juice	2 tbsp
1	pinch cinnamon	1
	freshly ground pepper and a little salt	
2	cloves garlic, chopped	2
125 mL	grated Pecorino or Romano cheese	½ cup

In an electric blender, combine the herbs with the Ricotta cheese to obtain a rich, creamy texture. If cream is too thick, add a little of the water used in cooking pasta. Add lemon juice, cinnamon, salt and pepper.

In a frying pan, sauté the garlic over very low heat. Do not allow to brown.

While preparing sauce, cook the pasta in salted boiling water. When it is *al dente,* serve with herb sauce mixed with garlic and Pecorino (or Romano) cheese.

371 calories per serving

MACARONI SURPRISE

(4 servings)

300 g	(600 mL) Catelli ready-cut macaroni	2½ cups
1	medium onion, grated	1
30 mL	olive oil	2 tbsp
3	medium zucchini, cut in round slices	3
125 mL	milk (2% M.F.) salt and pepper to taste	½ cup
250 mL	cottage cheese	1 cup
15 mL	breadcrumbs	1 tbsp
125 mL	feta cheese, broken into pieces	½ cup
1	egg, beaten	1
5 mL	oregano	1 tsp

Sauté the onion in olive oil until golden, then add the zucchini and cook for 5 minutes over low heat. Add 30 mL (2 tbsp) milk, with salt and pepper. Cover and allow to simmer 5 more minutes.

Meanwhile, cook the pasta in salted boiling water until half-done. Drain and add Ricotta cheese mixed with 15 mL (1 tbsp) milk.

Lightly grease an ovenproof dish, sprinkle with breadcrumbs and pour in half the pasta. Cover with zucchini over the whole surface. Add the remaining pasta and top with the Ricotta cheese mixed with the egg and the rest of the milk.

Place in a pre-heated oven at 180°C (350°F) and cook for about 30 minutes.

547 calories per serving

MACARONI OMELET

(4 servings)

200 g	(400 mL) Catelli ready-cut macaroni	1¾ cups
3	eggs	3
15 mL	skim milk (2% M.F.)	1 tbsp
45 mL	grated Parmesan cheese	3 tbsp
5 mL	tarragon	1 tsp
250 mL	tomato sauce	1 cup
	salt and pepper to taste	

Cook the pasta in salted boiling water. When it is *al dente*, drain and put aside.

Beat the eggs with the milk, Parmesan cheese and tarragon. Add salt and pepper. Mix with the pasta and pour into a teflon frying pan. Cook the omelet until golden on both sides.

Serve hot with tomato sauce.

291 calories per serving

SUNSHINE MACARONI

(4 servings)

300 g	(600 mL) Catelli ready-cut macaroni	2½ cups
50 mL	olive oil	¼ cup
	juice of 1 lemon	1
2	cloves garlic, crushed	2
	salt, pepper and oregano to taste	
4	bocconcini (mozzarella-style cheese ; can be found in Italian grocery stores)	4
3	ripe tomatoes, diced	3
125 mL	black olives, pitted	½ cup

To make sauce, combine the oil, lemon juice, garlic, salt, pepper and oregano. Add the bocconcini (cut into small pieces), the tomatoes and the olives.

Meanwhile, cook the pasta in salted boiling water. When it is *al dente*, drain and place in a salad bowl. Add sauce. Mix well but be careful not to break the macaroni.

Cool and serve on leaves of lettuce.

518 calories per serving

CRAB AU GRATIN

(4 servings)

320 g	(600 mL) Catelli ready-cut macaroni	2½ cups
250 g	frozen crab meat	½ lb
1	large onion, chopped	1
30 mL	olive oil	2 tbsp
	pepper to taste	
1	egg	1
250 mL	milk (2% M.F.)	1 cup
125 mL	grated mild cheddar cheese	½ cup
15 mL	breadcrumbs	1 tbsp

Sauté the onion in olive oil until golden, then add unfrozen crab meat. Stir quickly and add pepper to taste. Cover and allow to simmer.

Beat the egg with 75 mL (⅓ cup) milk, adding the cheese a little at a time. Put aside.

Meanwhile, cook the pasta in salted boiling water until half-done. Drain.

Lightly grease an ovenproof dish and sprinkle with bread-crumbs. Pour in half the pasta, then the crab, then the remaining pasta topped with the cheese mix. Pour the rest of the milk along the sides of the dish. Sprinkle with black pepper. Cook in a pre-heated oven at 200°C (400°F) for 35 minutes.

539 calories per serving

MACARONI WITH MIXED VEGETABLES

(4 servings)

320 g	(600 mL) Catelli ready-cut macaroni	2½ cups
250 mL	frozen small peas	1 cup
250 mL	frozen asparagus and carrots	1 cup
1	container (175 g) plain skim milk yogurt	1-6,5 oz
	juice of 1 lemon	1
15 mL	olive oil	1 tbsp
5 mL	dry mustard	1 tsp
1	clove garlic, crushed	1
	chopped parsley	
	a few chopped black olives	
	salt and pepper to taste	
4	cooked weiners, cut in round slices	4

Cook the macaroni in salted boiling water. When it is *al dente,* drain and rinse quickly in cold water.

Meanwhile, cook the vegetables in a little boiling water or chicken stock for more flavour. When they are done, drain and put aside.

To make the sauce, mix yogurt with lemon juice and olive oil. Beat vigorously and add the mustard, garlic, parsley and olives. Add salt and pepper.

Add sauce and vegetables to the macaroni, stirring well to make sure pasta is completely coated with the sauce.

At the end, add the slices of weiners. Place in a salad bowl and decorate with parsley.

Cool and serve.

516 calories per serving

Macaroni Omelet (page 93)
Baked Spinach Lasagne (page 112)

FUSILLI

Bolognese Macaroni Timbale (page 118)
Noodles Rockefeller (page 121)

FUSILLI TRIFOLATE

(4 servings)

300 g	(750 mL) Catelli fusilli springs	3 cups
250 mL	frozen mushrooms	1 cup
1	medium onion, grated	1
30 mL	olive oil	2 tbsp
4	small zucchini, cut in thin round slices	4
5 mL	oregano	1 tsp
	salt and pepper to taste	
1	egg	1
15 mL	milk	1 tbsp
30 mL	grated Parmesan cheese	2 tbsp

Get rid of excess moisture by allowing mushrooms to sweat for 30 minutes.

In a frying pan, sauté the onion in oil until golden, then add the zucchini, mushrooms and oregano. Add salt and pepper, cover, and allow to simmer over very low heat.

Beat the egg with milk and put aside.

Cook the pasta in salted boiling water. When it is *al dente,* drain and put back in pot over low heat.

Add vegetables and egg mixture to the pasta, sprinkle with Parmesan cheese and mix quickly.

Serve piping hot.

431 calories per serving

GARDENER'S FUSILLI

(4 servings)

320 g	(750 mL) Catelli fusilli springs	3 cups
250 mL	frozen small peas	1 cup
2	small onions, cut into pieces	2
250 mL	pippin apples, diced	1 cup
15 mL	unsalted butter	1 tbsp
250 mL	lean ham, diced	1 cup
	salt and pepper to taste	
1	pinch cinnamon	1
5 mL	oregano	1 tsp
50 mL	grated Parmesan cheese	¼ cup

Cook the peas, onions and apples in a little water. When tender, drain well and squeeze onions to remove water.

Add ham to vegetables and sauté in butter. Stir often and add a little water if needed. Add salt, pepper, cinnamon and oregano. Cover and allow to simmer for about 15 minutes over very low heat.

Meanwhile, cook the pasta in salted boiling water. When it is *al dente,* drain and stir in vegetable mixture. Top with Parmesan cheese and serve immediately.

503 calories per serving

FUSILLI WITH ROSEMARY

(4 servings)

300 g	(750 mL) Catelli fusilli springs	3 cups
1	medium onion, finely chopped	1
30 mL	olive oil	2 tbsp
225 g	lean chopped veal	½ lb
10 mL	flour	2 tsps
50 mL	chicken stock	¼ cup
	salt and pepper to taste	
15 mL	rosemary	1 tbsp

In a frying pan, sauté the onion in olive oil until golden. Add the veal, lightly dredged in flour, stirring constantly to prevent meat from sticking and to cook evenly. Then add the stock, salt and pepper, and rosemary at the very end. Cover and allow to simmer.

Meanwhile, cook the fusilli in salted boiling water. When they are *al dente,* drain and serve dressed with the sauce.

445 calories per serving

FUSILLI WITH ONIONS

(4 servings)

300 g	**(750 mL) Catelli fusilli springs**	3 cups
2	**large onions, finely sliced**	2
45 mL	**olive oil**	3 tbsp
	salt and pepper to taste	
60 mL	**grated Parmesan cheese, to taste**	4 tbsp

In a frying pan, sauté the onions in oil over low heat until translucent. Do not allow to brown. Add salt and pepper to taste.

Cook the pasta in salted boiling water. When it is *al dente*, drain and add onions and cheese. Serve immediately.

For a creamier sauce, add 30 mL (2 tbsp) Ricotta cheese diluted in a little skim milk or stock to the onions and cheese.

403 calories per serving

RAINBOWS

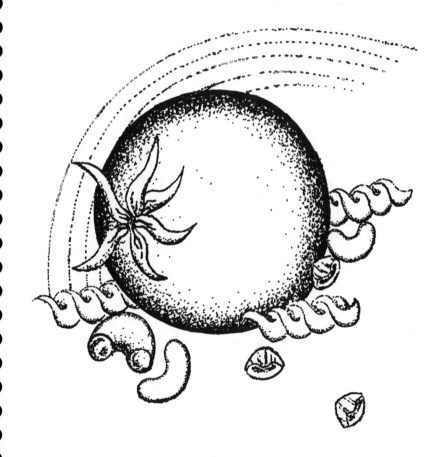

RAINBOW GALANTINE

(4 servings)

375 g	(500 mL) Catelli rainbows	2 cups
1	envelope (7 g) unflavoured gelatine	1
250 mL	water	1 cup
	juice of ½ lemon	½
3	cloves garlic, finely chopped	3
	salt and pepper to taste	
½	(175 g) container plain skim milk yogurt	½ - 6.5 oz
50 mL	celery, diced	¼ cup
250 mL	tomatoes, diced	1 cup
125 mL	carrots, grated	½ cup
125 mL	feta cheese, broken into pieces	½ cup
125 mL	parsley, finely chopped	½ cup
10 mL	oregano	2 tsp

Dissolve the gelatine in 75 mL (⅓ cup) cold water, then add 175 mL (⅔ cup) boiling water and lemon juice. Mix well. Add the garlic, salt and pepper.

Cook the pasta in salted boiling water. When it is done, drain and rinse in cold water.

In a large bowl, mix the yogurt and gelatine. Add the rainbows, celery, tomatoes, carrots, feta cheese, parsley and oregano. Mix well and pour into a mould. Place in the refrigerator and allow to set (about 3 hours).

Serve on leaves of lettuce or with the following sauce if preferred :

469 calories per serving

Sauce :

1	small container (175 g) plain skim milk yogurt	1 - 6.5 oz
3	cloves garlic, finely chopped	3
15 mL	olive oil	1 tbsp
	salt and pepper	

Beat yogurt and olive oil vigorously, then add the garlic, salt and pepper.

56 calories per serving

ALPHABETS

TOMATOES STUFFED WITH ALPHABETS

(4 servings)

150 g	(250 mL) Catelli alphabets	1 cup
30 mL	olive oil	2 tbsp
1	small can (184 g) tuna	1 - 6.5 oz
5 mL	oregano	1 tsp
	salt and pepper	
1	egg, beaten	1
4	large tomatoes, not too ripe	4
30 mL	grated cheddar cheese, mild or old	2 tbsp
4	black olives	4
1	bunch parsley	1

Sauté the onion in oil over low heat until golden. Do not allow to brown. Rinse tuna to remove excess oil and add to pan. Cover and allow to simmer for 10 minutes over very low heat.

Meanwhile, cook the alphabets in salted boiling water. When they are half-done, drain and allow to cool. Add egg, mix well and add the tuna fish.

Slice off tops and carefully hollow out the tomatoes, without breaking them. Turn tomatoes upside down and allow to sweat for 10 minutes. Then, fill the tomatoes with alphabets and tuna, sprinkle with cheese, put back tops and place in a pre-heated oven at 180°C (350°F) for 30 minutes.

Decorate with an olive and a sprig of parsley held down with a toothpick.

364 calories per serving

Variation : 100 g (¼ lb) veal can be used instead of tuna. Zucchini or green peppers can replace the tomatoes.

MUSSELS STUFFED WITH ALPHABETS

(4 servings)

150 g	(250 mL) Catelli alphabets	1 cup
3	dozen mussels	3 dozen
250 mL	water	1 cup
5 mL	garlic powder	1 tsp
1	bay leaf	1
15 mL	olive oil	1 tbsp
2	large tomatoes, diced	2
15 mL	tomato paste	1 tbsp
3	cloves garlic, crushed	3
	chopped parsley	
	salt and pepper to taste	
2	egg yolks	2

Wash the mussels thoroughly and place in cooking pot with 250 mL (1 cup) water, the garlic powder and bay leaf. Cook over high heat until the mussels open (about 5 minutes). When mussels are done, remove from cooking pot without breaking and reserve the cooking water.

Cook the alphabets in salted boiling water. When they are half-done, drain and add oil. Put aside.

In a frying pan, crush the tomatoes and cook over low heat. Add a little cooking water from the mussels, the tomato paste, garlic, parsley, salt and pepper.

Mix the alphabets, which have had time to cool, with the egg yolks. Stuff the mussels with the alphabets and place them side by side in an ovenproof dish. Pour the sauce and cook in a pre-heated oven at 200°C (400°F) for 25 minutes. Remove from oven, garnish with parsley.

298 calories per serving

109

LASAGNE

BAKED SPINACH LASAGNE

(4 servings)

340 g	(16 - 23 cm × 5 cm) Catelli spinach lasagne	16 - 9 × 2 inches
1	grated onion	1
30 mL	olive oil	2 tbsp
250 mL	Ricotta cheese	1 cup
125 mL	milk (2% M.F.)	½ cup
1	pinch ginger	1
5 mL	nutmeg	1 tsp
	salt and pepper to taste	
15 mL	raisins	1 tbsp
15 mL	pine nuts or almonds	1 tbsp
60 mL	grated Parmesan cheese	4 tbsp

Soak the raisins in a little water.

Sauté the onion in olive oil over low heat until translucent. Do not allow to brown. Add Ricotta cheese diluted in milk, then the ginger, nutmeg, salt and pepper. Cover and allow to simmer over very low heat. Add a little more milk if needed to prevent from sticking.

Cook the lasagne in salted boiling water. When it is half-done, drain. In a greased ovenproof dish, place a first layer of pasta, cover with sauce and sprinkle with nuts or almonds. Repeat the operation, alternating pasta and sauce. Cover last layer of pasta with sauce and sprinkle with Parmesan cheese. Place in a pre-heated oven at 200°C (400°F) and cook until top is golden brown (about 35 minutes).

553 calories per serving

LASAGNE CREOLE

(4 servings)

360 g	(14 - 23 cm × 5 cm) Catelli lasagne	14 - 9 × 2 in.
500 mL	water	2 cups
1	small onion	1
1	carrot	1
1	bay leaf	1
2	haddock fillets (180 g)	6 oz
1	medium onion, grated	1
15 mL	curry	1 tbsp
30 mL	olive oil	2 tbsp
250 mL	milk (2% M.F.)	1 cup
250 mL	Ricotta cheese	1 cup

Make a court-bouillon with the water, small onion, carrot and bay leaf, and poach the fish fillets. Water must get hot but not boil. Remove after 15 minutes.

Sauté the grated onion in oil for a few minutes and add the curry. Mix well, then add 15 mL (1 tbsp) milk. Place fish fillets in pan and turn a few times to coat them with the liquid. Cover and allow to simmer for 10 more minutes.

Cook the lasagne in salted boiling water. When it is half-done, remove from pot, being careful not to break it. In an ovenproof dish, place one layer of lasagne, then the fish fillets, and finally another layer of lasagne.

Mix the Ricotta cheese with the milk and curry sauce, and pour along the sides of the dish. Place in a pre-heated oven and cook at 200°C (400°F) for 30 minutes.

567 calories per serving

113

RECIPES FOR
SPECIAL OCCASIONS

TIMBALE MEDITERRANEAN-STYLE

(6 servings)

1	package of 500 g Catelli long macaroni	1
2	medium eggplants coarse salt flour	2
1	large onion	1
125 mL	crushed tomatoes	½ cup
10 mL	oregano	2 tsp
15 mL	wine vinegar	1 tbsp
500 mL	béchamel sauce	2 cup
50 mL	olive oil	¼ cup
250 g	ground beef salt and pepper to taste	½ lb
50 mL	grated Parmesan cheese	¼ cup
30 mL	breadcrumbs	2 tbsp

Wash and cut eggplants in slices, cover with coarse salt for a few hours to remove excess moisture. Pat dry eggplant slices, dice and dredge with a little flour.

Chop one half of the onion and sauté in olive oil over low heat. Add the eggplant and brown. When it is almost cooked, add the tomatoes, oregano and wine vinegar. Cover and allow to simmer.

Meanwhile, make a thick béchamel sauce and put aside.

Grate remaining half of the onion and sauté in a little oil. Add the ground beef, with salt and pepper.

Cook the pasta in salted boiling water until it is half-done, and drain. In a buttered timbale mould sprinkled with breadcrumbs, place a first layer of pasta, then a layer of ground beef, eggplant and béchamel sauce. Repeat operation, finishing with béchamel sauce. Sprinkle with Parmesan cheese and the remaining breadcrumbs.

Place in a pre-heated oven at 230°C (450°F) and cook for 20 minutes, then lower heat to 150°C (300°F) and cook 20 minutes more or until golden brown.

This recipe can be prepared the day before and warmed in the oven just before mealtime. It will only be more delicious, the flavours having had the time to blend together.

640 calories per serving

BOLOGNESE MACARONI TIMBALE

(8 servings)

600 g	(1 handful 8.5 cm in diameter) Catelli long macaroni	3½ inches in diameter
1	large onion, chopped	1
30 mL	olive oil	2 tbsp
100 g	ground pork	3.5 oz
100 g	ground beef	3.5 oz
500 mL	tomato sauce	2 cups
1	bay leaf	1
500 mL	béchamel sauce	2 cup
250 mL	small peas	1 cup
⅓	package filo leaves	⅓

Sauté the onion in oil and add pork and beef. Mix well. When meat is cooked, add tomato sauce and bay leaf. Allow to simmer for about 30 minutes over low heat.

Meanwhile, make the béchamel sauce and add peas.

Cook the pasta. When it is still firm to the bite, drain and mix with half the tomato sauce.

Butter a timbale mould and cover bottom and sides with 3 or 4 filo leaves. Cover with a layer of macaroni, then with béchamel and tomato sauce, then with another layer of 4 or 5 filo leaves. Repeat operation, finishing with 3 or 4 filo leaves. Seal the edges and brush well with oil.

Place timbale in a pre-heated oven at 200°C (400°F) and cook for about 45 minutes, then lower heat to 180°C (350°F) and cook for 10 minutes more. Remove from mould and serve with the sauce and Parmesan cheese.

572 calories per serving

LINGUINE FLAMBÉ

(6 servings)

This recipe is sure to win you the compliments of your guests. For a complete success, the serving dish must be very warm, as well as the pasta and the cognac.

½	package of 1 kg Catelli linguine	½
5 mL	crushed chili	1 tsp
50 mL	olive oil	¼ cup
1	medium onion, coarsely chopped	1
1	can (796 mL) tomatoes, crushed	1 - 28 oz
	salt to taste	
50 mL	cognac (or brandy)	¼ cup
125 mL	grated Pecorino cheese	½ cup

In a frying pan, sauté the chili and the onion in oil. When onion is golden, add tomatoes and salt, and allow to simmer for 30 minutes.

Meanwhile, cook the pasta *al dente*, drain well and put back in cooking pot over medium heat. Add cheese and half the cognac to the tomato sauce, and pour over the linguine, mixing well and quickly.

Transfer pasta immediately to a warm serving dish and pour remaining cognac. Flambé immediately. This last step may be done before your guests.

572 calories per serving

QUAIL DELIGHT

(6 servings)

600 g	(2.7 L) Catelli egg noodles	11¾ cups
4	quails	4
	a few dried cepe mushrooms	
1	small onion, chopped	1
50 mL	unsalted butter	¼ cup
50 mL	brandy	¼ cup
1	bay leaf	1
1	pinch ginger	1
	salt and pepper to taste	
125 mL	whipping cream	½ cup

Allow cepe mushrooms to soak in a little water for one hour. Reserve water. Cut quails in two, and press to flatten.

In a frying pan large enough to contain the four quails, sauté the onion in half the amount of butter until golden, then add the quails and cook until browned. Add the mushrooms, well drained, the brandy, ginger and bay leaf. Add a little water used to soak the mushrooms, if needed. Cover and allow to simmer for about 30 minutes over low heat. When quails are done, remove from pan, remove bones and chop up the meat. Put back in pan, add salt and pepper, cover and lower heat to a minimum.

Meanwhile, cook the noodles in salted boiling water. When they are *al dente,* drain well and add remaining butter. Heat the cream and pour over the pasta.

Serve the noodles topped with quail sauce.

686 calories per serving

NOODLES ROCKEFELLER

(6 servings)

600 g	(2.7 L) Catelli medium egg noodles	4¾ cups
6	slices (90 g) frozen smoked salmon	3 oz
1	chopped onion	1
15 mL	unsalted butter	1 tbsp
125 mL	white wine	½ cup
175 mL	whipping cream	¾ cup
	salt and pepper to taste	
1	small jar (28 g) black caviar	1 - 1 oz

Cut frozen slices of smoked salmon into fine strips.

Sauté the onion in butter then add the salmon, mixing well. Add white wine, cover and allow to simmer for 5 minutes over low heat. Remove cover and pour cream. Add very little salt (salmon is already salted) and pepper.

Cook the noodles in salted boiling water. When they are *al dente*, drain and put back in cooking pot. Add the sauce, and mix well, making sure the pasta does not stick to the pot.

Serve hot on warm plates. Garnish with caviar.

550 calories per serving

NOODLES WITH LEMON SAUCE

(6 servings)

This very delicate recipe calls for special care. Plates must be warmed before serving.

600 g	(2.7 L) Catelli egg noodles	11¾ cups
1	clove garlic	1
5 mL	butter	1 tsp
2	lemons	2
125 mL	light cream (15% M.F.)	½ cup
125 mL	milk	½ cup
	freshly ground pepper to taste	

Rub pan with garlic clove and melt butter. Add zest of two lemons and simmer over very low heat. Do not allow butter to brown.

Cook the noodles in salted boiling water. When they are still very *al dente*, drain well and put back in cooking pot. Pour the lemon-butter sauce, add salt and pepper and warm.

Serve piping hot on warm plates, with a dash of freshly ground black pepper if desired.

440 calories per serving

RIGATONI ALLA TORTA DI MASCARPONE

(6 servings)

Torta di Mascarpone is a delicious cheese made of a blend of Gorgonzola and Mascarpone cheese. It can be found in any Italian grocery store.

500 g	(1750 mL) Catelli rigatoni	7 cups
250 mL	torta di Mascarpone	1 cup
125 mL	milk	½ cup
125 mL	pistachios, finely chopped	½ cup
30 mL	marc or brandy	½ cup
15 mL	unsalted butter	2 tbsp
		1 tbsp

Mix the cheese and milk to obtain a rich, creamy texture. Add pistachios and marc (or brandy), and blend well.

Cook the rigatoni in salted boiling water. When it is very *al dente,* drain well and put back on the stove for no more than 2 minutes, adding the butter and the cheese. Mix quickly and serve piping hot on warm plates.

632 calories per serving

RIGATONI AND CHICKEN LIVER FEUILLETÉ

(8 servings)

600 g	**(2 L) Catelli rigatoni**	**8¾ cups**
1	**package (10 g) dried boletus mushrooms**	**0.5 oz**
1	**grated onion**	**1**
30 mL	**unsalted butter**	**2 tbsp**
150 g	**chicken livers**	**5 oz**
125 mL	**chicken stock**	**½ cup**
1	**bay leaf**	**1**
50 mL	**brandy**	**¼ cup**
500 mL	**béchamel sauce (made with water used to soak mushrooms)**	**2 cups**
	salt and pepper to taste	
⅓	**package filo leaves**	**⅓**
5 mL	**olive oil**	**1 tsp**

Soak the mushrooms in water for 1 hour, drain and reserve the water.

Sauté the onion in 15 mL (1 tbsp) butter. Add chicken livers and brown quickly with bay leaf over medium heat. Pour chicken stock and stir, then add brandy, cover and allow to simmer for 15 minutes over low heat.

Make a thick béchamel sauce with the water used to soak the mushrooms.

Cook the pasta in salted boiling water. Meanwhile, lightly grease a deep, round timbale mould and place 5 filo leaves at the bottom and on the sides of the mould. When pasta is half-done, drain well and add the mushrooms, béchamel sauce, chicken livers cut into pieces, and the remaining butter. Mix well and pour one layer in mould. Cover with 5 more filo leaves and repeat operation, alternating layers of sauce and of filo leaves. Finish with 3 or 4 filo leaves and seal the edges. Brush with oil.

Place in a pre-heated oven at 200°C (400°F) and cook for about 45 minutes.

Serve with the following sauce.

Chicken liver sauce

50 g	chicken liver	2 oz
15 mL	flour	1 tbsp
10 mL	butter	2 tsp
50 mL	chopped onion	¼ cup
50 mL	chicken stock	¼ cup
1	crushed bay leaf	1
5 mL	olive oil	1 tsp
5 mL	brandy	1 tsp

Sauté the chicken livers in 5 mL (1 tsp) butter and purée in an electric blender.

Make a roux with the flour and butter, add the stock, bay leaf, the onion sautéed in oil, and the brandy. Combine chicken liver purée.

Serve piping hot on the timbale.

493 calories per serving

126

BUTTERFLIES BELLEVUE

(6 servings)

500 g	(1,9 L) Catelli medium bows	7⅔ cups
1	small onion, finely chopped	1
5 mL	unsalted butter	1 tsp
30 mL	Ricotta cheese	2 tbsp
250 mL	fresh whipping cream	1 cup
1	lemon	1
2	small jars (28 g) black caviar	2 - 1 oz
	salt and pepper to taste	

Sauté the onion in a little butter over very low heat until golden. Do not allow to brown. Mix onion with Ricotta cheese and add cream a little at a time. Add grated zest of the lemon and place over very low heat.

Cook the pasta in salted boiling water. When it is *al dente,* drain and dress with the sauce, mixing well for about 30 seconds over very low heat.

Add the caviar and combine carefully with the pasta.

Serve immediately on warm plates and decorate each plate with a little caviar and a thin slice of lemon.

This very delicate recipe must be prepared with care and the serving plates must be warm.

484 calories per serving

TIMBALE ROYALE

(8 servings)

600 g	(2 L) Catelli rigatoni	8¾ cups
12	clams	12
12	large prawns	12
24	mussels	24
500 mL	water	2 cups
1	stalk celery	1
1	carrot, diced	1
1	clove garlic	1
1	bay leaf	1
750 mL	béchamel sauce prepared with the water in which the sea food was cooked	3 cups
1	small onion, grated	1
15 mL	olive oil	1 tbsp
50 mL	white wine (or pastis, if you like)	¼ cup
	salt and pepper to taste	
100 g	crab meat	3.5 oz
⅓	of package filo leaves	⅓
15 mL	unsalted butter	1 tbsp

Wash the seafood (clams, prawns, mussels) thoroughly. Make a court-bouillon : in a pot containing 500 mL (2 cups) water, add the seafood, celery, carrot, garlic and bay leaf. Cook at a rapid boil, at first, then over medium heat and uncovered to reduce court-bouillon. When seafood is done (about 7 to 10 minutes), remove from pot with a strainer and remove shells.

With the court-bouillon, make a béchamel sauce that is light but not too thin.

Sauté the onion in oil, then add the seafood and crab meat.

Mix well and add wine. Allow to simmer for 10 minutes over low heat, then add one half of the béchamel sauce.

Meanwhile, cook the rigatoni in salted boiling water. When it is half-done, drain and add butter.

In a greased timbale mould, place 4 or 5 lightly oiled filo leaves, then add one layer of rigatoni and one layer of sea-food. Cover with 3 or 4 more filo leaves, lightly oiled, and repeat operation, alternating rigatoni and seafood. Finish by covering with 4 or 5 filo leaves. Seal the edges and brush with oil.

Place in a pre-heated oven at 180°C (350°F) and cook for about 55 minutes. Remove from mould and decorate with a few mussels and prawns. Serve hot with remaining bécha-mel sauce, thinned with a little court-bouillon if needed.

555 calories per serving

FUSILLI FORNARINA

(6 servings)

The following recipe is very easy to make. However, the sauce must absolutely remain warm. We therefore recommend that the plates be warmed before serving.

500 g	(1,25 L) Catelli fusilli	5 cups
150 g	Gorgonzola cheese	5 oz
1	egg	1
125 mL	fresh whipping cream	½ cup
	a little milk, if needed	
125 mL	chopped walnuts	½ cup
125 mL	chopped pistachios	½ cup
1	pinch nutmeg	1
50 mL	unsalted butter	¼ cup

In a bowl, gently crush the cheese with a spatula. Add the egg and combine well, adding the cream a drop at a time. If the mixture is still too thick, add a little milk to obtain a rich, creamy texture.

Crush the walnuts and pistachios together in a mortar. (If you do not have a mortar, a wooden spoon wrapped in cloth may be used. Crush the nuts with back of spoon.) Combine nuts to cheese and add nutmeg.

Cook the pasta in salted boiling water. When it is *al dente*, drain and put back in cooking pot over very low heat. Add the sauce and the butter, mix very quickly and serve immediately.

654 calories per serving

COUNTRY-STYLE MACARONI

(6 servings)

400 g	(800 mL) Catelli ready-cut macaroni	3½ cups
4	slices of bacon, coarsely chopped	4
4	slices of ham, coarsely chopped	4
250 mL	small peas	1 cup
1	large onion, chopped	1
4	eggs	4
125 mL	chopped parsley	½ cup
500 mL	tomato sauce	2 cups

In a frying pan, sauté the bacon, ham and onion. When bacon is crisp, add peas.

In a bowl, beat the eggs and add parsley.

Cook the pasta in salted boiling water. When it is very *al dente*, drain and put back in cooking pot. Add tomato sauce, eggs and meat, onion and pea mixture. Place over low heat and mix well. Serve piping hot on warm plates.

429 calories per serving

GLOSSARY OF INGREDIENTS

ANCHOVY : Small sea fish, salted and marinated in oil. An anchovy paste is also available, sold in small tubes.

ANETH : This herbaceous plant is easier to find during the pickling season, in markets or in food stores. You can always use aneth seeds, which are available in the spice section. You can obtain a powder by crushing the seeds.

ARTICHOKE HEARTS : Any well supplied grocer will be able to sell you canned artichoke hearts.

BASIL : This aromatic plant can be found during the summer, at the market and in all grocery stores.

BEET LEAVES : Looks like spinach but has a more refined taste. Seasonal, it can be found in many supermarkets.

CAPERS : Marinated in vinegar they make a very good condiment and seasoning. You usually find them on the imported products shelf at larger grocery stores.

CEPE MUSHROOMS (Dried) : This mushroom is picked in Europe, imported and sold through delicatessen shops. It is difficult to replace, because of it's very special finesse and taste.

CHILI PEPPER : Red, dried and hot, can be found at the spice counter, it is more convenient to buy them already crushed.

CORIANDER : The strong taste of this spice may not please all unanimously, some prefer the milder savory. Look for it in the spice section at grocery stores.

CURRY : Spice from India. It's yellow color makes it easily identifiable. It is mainly sold as a powder.

FENNEL : When buying the whole plant you may consume the bulb as a vegetable and use the leaves as seasoning. Expect to find it during the pickling season only.

FILO PASTE : Traditionally used in mediterranean and middle-eastern cooking. Baklavas are one example. Contains very little calories. Now mass produced in our country it can be found mainly in fruit and vegetable stores and if not, at specialized import stores.

MARC : Normally made of pressed grapes ; it can be replaced by any type of brandy.

OLIVES, GREEK OR BLACK : Marinated in vinegar, imported from the "warm countries" and kept in large trays at the fruit and vegetable counter of some supermarkets or in delicatessen shops.

OLIVE OIL : Universally sold. May be replaced by corn or sunflower oil, yet with a difference.

PINE KERNEL : Can be found in delicatessen and import stores. May be replaced in recipes with almonds.

PIPPIN APPLES : If not in stock at your grocer's because of the season, use green apples.

SAFFRON : Orange powder used as a colouring rather than a seasoning. Look for it in delicatessens or Spanish import stores.

SMOKED SALMON : To be purchased in very thin layers. Smoked salmon is pink and orange in colour and has a delicate and refined flavour. Can be found in supermarkets at the fish market.

SNOW-PEAS : Green vegetable resembling a green bean that has been delicately flattened. Available frozen year round or fresh in the springtime. The Chinese love them.

CALORIE CHART

INGREDIENTS	QUANTITY	CALORIES
Pasta	one 85g serving (3 oz)	306

VEGETABLES :

artichokes (canned)	4	63
asparagus	one 341 mL can (12 oz)	41
eggplant	1	86
carrot	1 medium	20
celery	1 stick	5
dried mushrooms	10 g (0.5 oz)	25
fresh mushrooms	250 mL (1 cup)	28
cauliflower	1 small	79
Brussel sprouts	12	87
zucchini	1	36
fresh spinach	142 g (5 oz)	35
onion	1 medium	40
leek	1	66
frozen peas	125 g (¼ lb)	91
canned peas	125 mL (½ cup)	59
green pepper	1	15
tomato	1	35
tomatoes	one 540 mL can (19 oz)	114
tomato sauce	250 mL (1 cup)	100

SEAFOOD :

anchovies	5 filets	35
shrimps	250g (½ lb)	228
mussels	36	314
smoked salmon	90 g (3 oz)	64
tuna	one 184 g can (6.5 oz)	361
smoked trout	155 g (5 oz)	334

MEATS :

lamb	200 g (6.5 oz)	675
lean ground beef	250 g (½ lb)	448
ham	120 g (¼ lb)	275
chicken	2-200 g breasts (6,5 oz)	300
lean ground veal	200 g (6,5 oz)	346

DAIRY PRODUCTS :

butter	15 mL (1 tbsp)	100
light cream (15%)	125 mL (½ cup)	247
whipped cream	250 mL (1 cup)	869
cheddar cheese	30 mL (2 tbsp)	56
cottage cheese (4% BF)	125 mL (½ cup)	122
feta cheese	125 mL (½ cup)	330
gorgonzola cheese	125 mL (½ cup)	150
gruyere cheese	125 mL (½ cup)	178
mozzarella cheese	125 mL (½ cup)	252
parmesan cheese	30 mL (2 tbsp)	64
ricotta cheese	125 mL (½ cup)	216
romano cheese	125 mL (½ cup)	290
skim milk (2%)	250 mL (1 cup)	129
skim milk yogourt	one 175 g container (6,5 oz)	98

CONDIMENTS :

almonds	125 mL (½ cup)	359
capers	125 mL (½ cup)	85
olive oil	15 mL (1 tbsp)	125
black olives	2	15
white sauce prepared with milk	250 mL (1 cup)	428

ALCOHOL :

brandy	5 mL (1 tsp)	12
white wine	50 mL (¼ cup)	40

NOTES

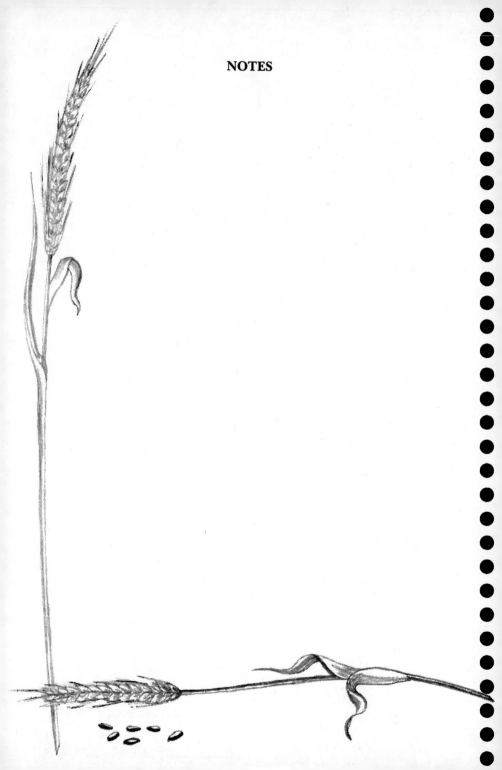

NOTES

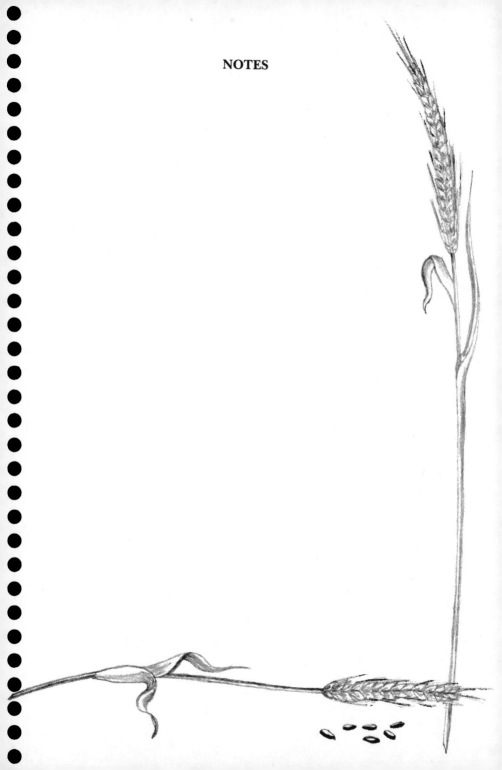

NOTES

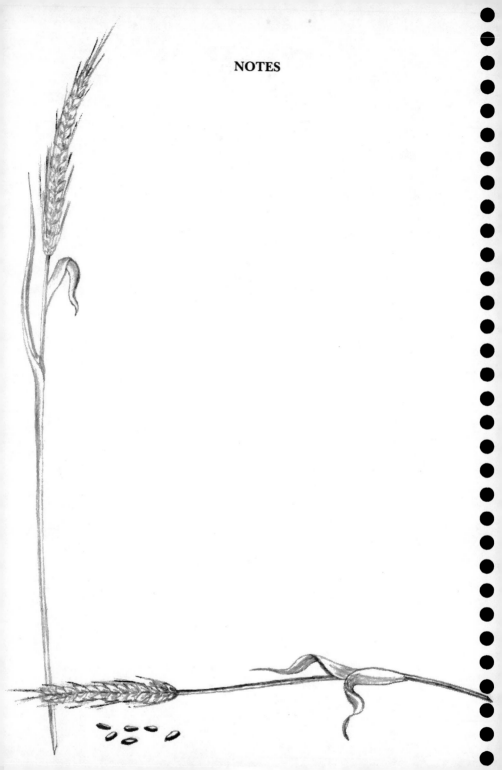

NOTES

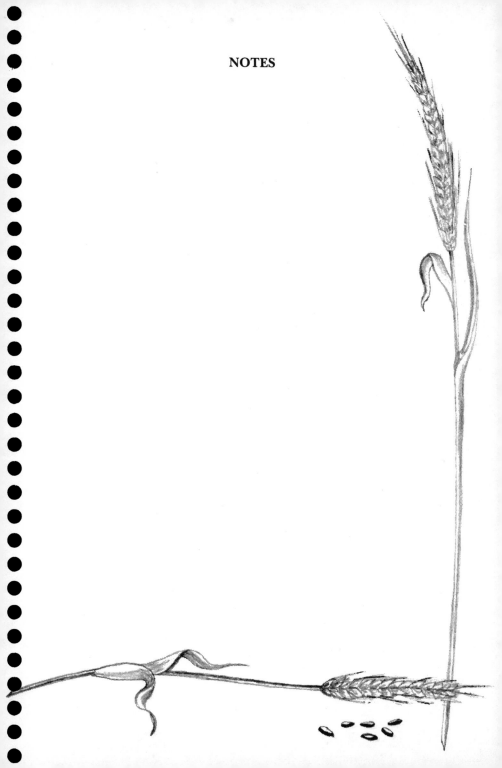

Printed in Canada